SKILLS REAL MEN SHOULD KNOW

How to Start a Fire, Change a Tire, Drive With a Trailer, Perform CPR, Setup a Campsite, Catch a Fish, and Many More!

JACK FENN

ISBN: 978-1-962496-10-0

For questions, please reach out to Support@OakHarborPress.com

Please consider leaving a review!
Just visit: OakHarborPress.com/Reviews

FREE BONUS

SCAN ME!

GET OUR NEXT BOOK FOR FREE!
Scan or go to:
OakHarborPress.com/Free

Table of Contents

INTRODUCTION

In a world where technological advancements are rapidly changing the way we live and work, it's easy to overlook the value of fundamental skills that every man should possess. From basic navigation to breaking down a door, there are certain skills that are essential for every man to master in order to lead a successful and fulfilling life. Whether you're a young man just starting out on your journey or a seasoned adult looking to enhance your skill set, this book is designed to provide practical advice and guidance on the most important skills every man should know. With a focus on real-world scenarios, this book will help you develop the skills necessary to succeed in today's ever-changing world.

This book is not about teaching you how to be the perfect man or how to fit into society's definition of masculinity. Rather, it's about equipping you with the tools and knowledge you need to navigate life's challenges with confidence and competence.

The sections in this book cover a wide range of topics from basic survival skills to financial management. You'll learn how to change a tire, tie a tie, negotiate a salary, and much more.

This book is designed as a jumping-off point to develop different habits and skill sets. Although many of the sections are brief tutorials, they were created to inspire you to master the skills that best suit your needs. By exploring your strengths, weaknesses, and values, you'll be better equipped to make decisions that align with your goals and aspirations.

Ultimately, the purpose of this book is to empower you to live a fulfilling life by mastering the essential skills every man should know. Whether you're looking to build your confidence, expand your knowledge, or simply become more self-sufficient, this book is a valuable resource that will help you achieve your objective.

PADDLE A CANOE

THUMB
PERPENDICULAR
TO CANOE

PADDLE
ENTERS
VERTICALLY

THUMB
POINTS
TO WATER

PADDLE
SLICES WATER

Learning to use a canoe can be a valuable and rewarding way to connect with nature. Mastering canoeing techniques and skills will instill a sense of accomplishment and confidence. To find the right canoe for you, consider your plans and the number of passengers you want to bring along on your adventures. Most recreational sports stores will have knowledgeable staff who can help you choose the right size and weight for your needs. When loading the canoe, it's important to keep your gear evenly distributed since canoes can easily become unbalanced and tip. It's also important to invest in proper personal flotation devices before leaving on a trip.

When climbing in, step into the center of the canoe, keeping your weight low and centered. The J-stroke is a fundamental technique to learn for maintaining direction and control while paddling. Here's how to perform it:

> **Sit in the canoe.** Hold your paddle with one hand gripping the top and the other gripping the shaft just above the blade.
>
> **Dip the paddle into the water** on the opposite side from the direction you want to turn your canoe. The blade of the paddle should enter the water well in front of your knees. This is called the "catch" of your stroke.
>
> **Pull the paddle toward you,** keeping it vertical and parallel to the canoe. This will cause the canoe to turn in the opposite direction of the paddle.
>
> **When the paddle blade reaches your hip,** twist your wrist and turn the blade parallel to the canoe.
>
> **Push the paddle away from you** and away from the canoe so that it creates a J shape in the water. This will help keep the canoe on a straight path.

Repeat the stroke on the opposite side of the canoe to maintain the canoe's direction.

As you practice the J-stroke, think of your paddle as a lever that you're pulling to deliver a powerful, smooth motion through the water. The paddle's shaft acts as a fulcrum, or pivot point, for the lever so that you can get the fullest, most efficient stroke possible.

NAVIGATE

Navigation may seem irrelevant given today's technology, but most devices won't work in remote areas where cell phone coverage is limited. There are also emergency circumstances where you could find yourself without any access to technology, especially if you spend time exploring the wilderness. Knowing how to navigate using simple tools can help keep you and your loved ones safe. This skill is also extremely helpful for many professional careers including search and rescue, military service, and working as a wilderness guide. The basic tools for navigation are a map and compass. Today, you can purchase all kinds of gadgets that come with a compass built into them, ranging from watches to flashlights and even jewelry. Keeping maps in your glove compartment or backpack is a good practice to ensure you can always find your way.

For basic navigation:

Start by orienting your map. This means aligning your map with the surrounding landscape, looking for prominent features such as mountains, ridges, waterways, and trails.

Determine your heading. Use the compass to determine your heading, or direction of travel. Align the compass with the map by placing the base plate of the compass along the direction of travel on the map. Rotate the compass housing until the magnetic needle aligns with the orienting arrow on the base plate.

Set your course. Determine the angle of your desired course by rotating the compass housing until the desired bearing aligns with the direction-of-travel arrow on the base plate.

Follow your course. Hold the compass level in front of you and follow your course by keeping the magnetic needle aligned with the orienting arrow on the base plate. Keep the direction-of-travel arrow pointed in the desired direction of travel.

Check your progress. Periodically check your progress by identifying landmarks or other features on the map and comparing them to your surroundings. This will help you stay on course. Adjust your route if necessary.

Once you master basic navigation using a map and compass, it's a good idea to learn more in-depth skills, such as how to triangulate your location based off landmarks, for moments where it's difficult to figure out where you are. Remember that the best way to feel confident navigating in an emergency is to practice these skills frequently before you need to use them.

THROW A PUNCH

While we would never advocate for violence, there are moments when knowing how to properly throw a punch without hurting yourself is necessary. Without proper form, throwing a punch can injure your hand, sometimes enough to break fingers or bones, which can drastically decrease your ability to protect yourself during a confrontation.

Get in a fighter's stance. Place your feet shoulder-width apart and face your target with your nondominant foot in front of you at a 45-degree angle relative to your opponent. Your dominant foot should be behind you and pointed away from your target.

Make a proper fist by tightly closing your hand and placing your thumb over your four fingers; the tip of your thumb should be resting on your middle finger's knuckle. Do *not* tuck your thumb under your fingers, as this is the recipe for a broken hand.

Keep your fist tightly closed and your wrist lined up straight with your forearm. Otherwise, you'll likely end up spraining your wrist.

Tuck your dominant fist against your chin and keep your nondominant fist out front as a guard.

Slightly bend your knees to stabilize yourself and generate power.

Pivot your back foot and turn your back knee inward to initiate the punch. Your legs might dip down a bit when you do this, but that will help increase the power of your punch.

Twist your hips and chest toward your opponent and allow your dominant hand to follow your chest as you turn.

Extend your fist and keep your forearm pointed upward as you transfer your energy from your back foot to your front foot.

Strike your target with your middle knuckle and follow through.

Once you reach your full extension, snap your body back into your original fighter's stance to prepare for a response.

SET UP A CAMPSITE

Whether you're an avid camper or you only go when you have to, knowing how to select and set up a campsite is a sure way to impress your friends, family members, or a prospective life partner. The key to setting up a comfortable, organized, and safe campsite is having the right gear. You don't need to spend a lot of money on gear if you plan ahead. If you shop toward the end of summer, you will usually find gear at garage sales and second-hand stores, and sports retail centers will have items for sale at a discount. Keeping an eye on online marketplaces can also help you find good gear at decent prices to get you set up.

To select a campsite, find a flat surface free of rocks, roots, and uneven protrusions. The best location will have a slight slope or hill with a flat top; this will provide a route for rain to flow, which can prevent your site from becoming waterlogged. Having trees nearby is extremely helpful as well, as they can provide protection from wind and sun. They are also helpful for stringing up tarps for extra protection. In addition, you should choose a spot that's near a water source (even if it's man made) and within 200 feet of a bathroom. If there's no bathroom available, you can dig a small pit 200 feet away from your site and water source to bury your waste.

Once your site is chosen, it's a good idea to collect soft foliage such as dried grass and leaves to layer beneath your tent. This will help provide insulation between you and the ground, which is important for keeping warm once the temperature drops at night.

Remove any sticks or hard protrusions from this pile, and cover it with a tarp for added protection.

Tent setup will vary depending on what kind you have. Directions are often listed on the bag or in a small sheet included with the product. However, in general, there are poles, stakes, and the main canvas body of the tent.

Start by spreading the base of the tent over your insulation layer and use stakes to anchor it with the loops provided around the base. The base should be taut with the stakes anchored at an angle facing the interior of the tent. Sometimes, tough ground can make this difficult, so use a rock to help if needed.

Assemble your poles and then slide them through the hoops, clips, ties, or openings along the top of the tent.

Once the poles are secured to the top of the tent, bend and secure them to the small metal pieces found either at the corners of your tent or on the stakes.

Once your tent is set up, you can use the trees around you to string up a tarp at an angle over the tent to provide additional protection from the elements. Tying it at an angle will allow water to slide off in the direction you desire.

You can also create a wall with a third tarp to use as a wind block if you don't have trees surrounding your campsite.

Your campsite should always be clean and well organized, not just because it's more comfortable that way, but also because it's safer. If you leave trash and food around your campsite, wild animals will be drawn to your location. To avoid a dangerous encounter with these animals:

Designate a place for trash and recycling that is at least 20 feet from your campsite and unreachable by local wildlife.

Keep your food in bags and hang them in a location that is at least 200 feet from your campsite and 10–12 feet off the ground.

Establish your cooking fire or stove so that it's downwind to avoid enticing animals.

Transport your food to and from your campsite in appropriate coolers and containers.

Use provided trash receptacles when possible, as they are animal proof (or at least resistant).

Before building a campfire, make sure there are no open fire bans in effect. If it's safe to build a fire, keep it at least 15 feet from any flammable vegetation and your tents. Leave a bucket of water and shovel nearby to extinguish the fire, and keep wind direction in mind so that your tents aren't in danger if a gust of wind kicks up. Use twigs, dry leaves, grass, and needles for tinder and dead wood for fuel and kindling.

PUT OUT A FIRE

There are more than 350,000 house fires every year in the United States alone, so knowing how to put one out could save your home or even your life. If a fire extinguisher is available, you can use it to put out small fires that are still in their incipient stages. Follow the instructions on the extinguisher, which will tell you to pull the pin, aim at the base of the fire, squeeze the lever slowly and evenly, and move the nozzle in a sweeping motion.

If you don't have a fire extinguisher, get one. If a fire occurs before then, use the following strategies to put it out. Not all fires are the same, so it's important to learn multiple strategies. However, you should only attempt to put out a fire that's still in its beginning stages before it gets out of control.

Cooking fires:

Cover a small cooking fire with a metal cooking lid or cookie sheet. Keep the cover in place until it's cool to the touch.

Use a fire blanket to cover a fire and smother it. The blanket must be made of fiberglass or another flame-resistant material.

Don't swat at the flames. This creates airflow, which feeds oxygen to the fire and will make it worse.

Pour a large amount of baking soda or salt on the fire. *Do not* pour flour on the fire.

Turn off all heat sources.

Electrical fires:

If it's safe, **unplug the item that's causing the fire.**

Cut the electricity at the house breaker panel.

Pour baking soda on the fire to smother it.

Do *not* pour water on an electrical fire.

Other fires:

These fires include those that involve wood, paper, trash, plastic, or clothing.

Fill a bucket with water and pour it over the flames.

If you're trying to put out a fire in a wood-burning fireplace, pour baking soda over the flames or spread out the logs and embers to remove the fuel.

PREDICT THE WEATHER

Predicting the weather isn't easy, but there are some tricks to knowing whether you'll need your overcoat or your flip flops when you're headed out for the day. Clouds are the most reliable indicator of weather, at least without knowledge of the factors that meteorologists rely on, such as wind speed, atmospheric pressure, and so on.

White, wispy clouds that are high in the sky usually mean the weather will be clear.

Fluffy clouds mean the air is unstable, while **flat clouds** indicate stability.

Small, puffy clouds will usually accumulate into storm clouds throughout the day.

Dark, low clouds indicate rain or snow depending on the air temperature.

Clouds that are high in the sky early in the day can drop lower as the day progresses, so keep an eye on them to predict weather changes.

Pay attention to the movement of the clouds, as the direction the clouds are moving will tell you if a storm is coming in.

Lowering clouds mean a storm is on its way, while rising clouds mean the weather is clearing.

Aside from clouds, paying attention to the sky's color can clue you into what weather to expect. If the morning sky is red, it means the weather in the east is clear, but the weather in the west is bad. This is because weather moves from west to east, while the sun moves from east to west. It's the nugget of truth in the old adage, "Red sky at night, sailors delight; red skies in morning, sailors take warning."

BREAK DOWN
A DOOR

HOW TO BREAK DOWN A DOOR

KICK NEAR LOCK, NOT LOCK ITSELF

LEAN INTO KICK

DRIVE HEEL INTO DOOR

DRIVE HEEL OF STANDING FOOT INTO GROUND

Knowing how to break down a door is a skill that everyone should know, not just men. Whether you need to escape from a locked room or help loved ones trapped during a fire, mastering this skill can come in handy during emergency situations.

To break down a door:

Check the direction the door opens by examining the hinges. Doors that open inward are much easier to break down than those that open outward.

Do not use your shoulder.

Do not use a jump kick.

Stand back from the door a short distance.

Raise your dominant leg and kick right beside the lock, driving your kicking heel into the door while your other foot drives into the ground.

Do not kick the lock itself, as that's a good way to injure your foot.

Repeat the kicking motion. The wood should begin to splinter and eventually break away from the jamb.

FILTER WATER

As you're aware, you can't live long without water. However, even running water can carry bacteria and small organisms that can make you extremely sick, which is why it's a good idea to learn how to filter any water you plan to drink or cook with.

You can create a basic filter with a plastic water bottle using these steps:

- Cut the wide bottom end of the water bottle off.
- In this order, layer rocks, gravel, debris (e.g., small leaves and twigs), and sand. If you have charcoal, you should add some since it can help clean the water.
- You can add a mesh layer to the top or even use a sock in a pinch.
- Pour the water through this filter; it will come out of the spout significantly clearer than before.

After this process, you'll want to boil your water for at least two minutes. If you are planning on going camping or adventuring in places where you may need to purify your own water, consider purchasing disinfectant tablets or UV lights specifically designed to kill anything in the water without boiling it.

START A FIRE

It may seem easy to start a fire with access to lighters and matches, but there are many factors that can cause a fire to go out or prevent it from catching in the first place. To begin with, you'll need to gather the right materials. At the bare minimum, you'll need small sticks, dry grass and leaves, and logs or larger branches. If possible, obtain matches and/or a lighter to make things easier. You should also gather some large rocks to make a fire pit and have a bucket of water or sand nearby to suffocate the fire when needed.

Once you've gathered all your materials, you're ready to start a fire. Follow these next steps:

Choose a safe location. Select an area that's clear of dry grass, leaves, and other flammable materials. A fire pit or fire ring is an excellent option if one is available.

Gather materials. You'll need three types of materials to build a fire: tinder, kindling, and fuel. Tinder is small, dry material that catches fire easily such as dry leaves, grass, or wood shavings. Kindling is slightly larger material that burns longer and hotter than tinder such as small sticks or twigs. Fuel is the larger wood that sustains the fire such as logs or branches.

Build the base. Create a small pile of tinder in the center of your fire pit or cleared area. Make sure the tinder is loosely piled so that air can circulate through it.

Add kindling. Lay the kindling over the top of the tinder in a crisscross pattern, allowing spaces for air to flow through and the fire to breathe.

Light the tinder. Use a match or lighter to ignite the tinder. If the wind is blowing, hold the match or lighter on the downwind side of the tinder.

If you don't have matches or a lighter, cut a V-shaped notch in a flat piece of wood and place tiny bits of bark inside as kindling. Find a round stick and place the end of it in the notch. Place your palms on either side of the stick and roll it back and forth to create friction. When the stick the bark begins to burn and smolder, transfer the coal to the dry grass and leaves in your fire pit.

Add fuel. As the kindling catches fire, gradually add larger pieces of fuel to the fire. Make sure you don't smother the fire with too much material.

Maintain the fire. Once the fire is burning well, you need to maintain it. Ensure that the fire has enough fuel without blocking the flow of air.

Remember to always keep an eye on your fire, and never leave it unattended. When you're finished with your fire, extinguish it completely by pouring water or sand over it and stirring the ashes until they're cool to the touch.

SWIM

As with many of the skills listed here, swimming is essential for everyone, not just men. Even if you purposely avoid water, there may be instances where you absolutely can't escape it, and knowing how to swim can save your life or someone else's. For instance, what if you have a car accident and end up in a lake? It could happen, and the best way to survive that scenario is to know how to swim.

Learning to swim begins with getting comfortable in the water. In the shallow end of a pool or the shore edge of a lake, gradually lower yourself into the water until you're able to fully immerse your head. Doing this in shallow water ensures you can stand up if you panic.

Practice floating on your back. Human bodies are naturally buoyant, and being on your back keeps your face out of the water, allowing you to relax more than if you were on your stomach. If you're in a pool, practice floating near the edge at first so that you can hold onto the side. As you grow more comfortable, turn over on your stomach and practice the front float. Gradually move away from the sides as you become comfortable with floating.

Practice blowing bubbles in the shallow end of a pool. This will teach you breath control for when your face is underwater. When you swim, you inhale through the mouth when your face is above water and exhale through your nose when your face is below water. Blowing bubbles gets you used to this pattern.

Practice kicking while holding the side of the pool with your hands. The flutter kick, in which you keep your legs as straight as possible and alternate lifting them out of and placing them back in the water, is the most popular type of kick for beginners.

Add arm strokes while you're floating to propel you through the water. The backstroke is the easiest to learn, but the front stroke will get you where you're going faster.

PERFORM CPR

Knowing how to perform cardiopulmonary resuscitation (CPR) is a life-saving skill that can come in handy on even the most unassuming days. Situations where someone's breathing or heart stops can arise anywhere, anytime.

Check for responsiveness. First, try to wake the person up by tapping their shoulders and calling their name. If there's no response, shout for help.

Call emergency services. If someone is with you, ask them to call emergency services immediately while you begin CPR. If you're alone, call emergency services first before starting CPR.

Position the person by laying them face up on a flat, firm surface.

Open the person's airway. Gently tilt their head back with one hand while lifting their chin with the other.

Check for breathing by placing your ear near the person's mouth and nose. If they're not breathing or are breathing abnormally, you need to start CPR.

Perform chest compressions by placing the heel of one hand in the center of the person's chest between the nipples. Place your other hand on top of the first and interlock your fingers. Press down firmly and quickly about 2 inches deep, at a rate of 100–120 compressions per minute. Allow the chest to recoil fully between compressions. The goal of these compressions is to pump blood to the heart, which is why it's important to press and lift at the proper tempo. Most courses advise singing the song "Staying Alive" to keep the rhythm at the correct pace.

Perform rescue breaths by tilting the head back and lifting the person's chin again. Pinch their nose shut and blow two slow breaths into the person's mouth, watching for the chest to rise each time.

Continue CPR. Alternate between 30 compressions and two breaths until emergency services arrive or the person begins breathing on their own.

Although these are the basics, it's important to receive CPR training from a certified instructor to ensure you're performing CPR correctly. Remember to stay calm and focused and call for help immediately in any emergency situation.

HUNT

Hunting can be a challenging and rewarding activity for those who enjoy spending time in the great outdoors. This skill can take years to hone, and practice is necessary to become competent and confident. These tips won't guarantee you'll catch an animal as hunting requires proper preparation, knowledge, and skills, but here are some general steps to consider when planning a hunting trip:

Check regulations. Before going hunting, make sure to check the hunting regulations in your area. You may need to obtain a hunting license, permits, and/or tags to hunt certain animals.

Obtain the right equipment. Having the right equipment is essential for a successful hunt. Make sure you have appropriate clothing, boots, firearms or bows, ammunition, knives, and any other hunting gear you may need.

Scout the area prior to your trip to identify potential hunting spots, water sources, animal trails, and feeding areas. This can increase your chances of success.

Learn about animal behavior. Understanding the behavior and habits of the animals you're hunting can increase your chances of a successful hunt. Research their diet, habitat, and movement patterns. Learning to identify tracks can help you find a good place to wait for game.

Be patient and stay still. Hunting requires patience and stillness. Once you've located a good spot, wait quietly and patiently for the animals to come to you. Avoid making noise or sudden movements that could scare them away.

Take safety precautions. Hunting can be dangerous, so it's important to take safety precautions. Always wear protective clothing and follow firearm safety rules. Hunt with a partner, if possible, and make sure someone knows where you are and when you expect to return.

Respect the environment. Hunting should be done with respect for the environment and the animals being hunted. Always follow ethical hunting practices and never take more animals than you need.

It's important to note that hunting laws and regulations can vary greatly depending on the location and type of animal being hunted. Always research and follow local regulations and guidelines, and consider taking a hunting safety course or seeking guidance from an experienced hunter. A mentor can help you become more efficient at hunting. You can find a mentor by exploring online groups and forums or keeping an eye out for bulletin boards in community centers and sports retail stores for leads.

CATCH A FISH

Using a rod and reel is the easiest way to catch a fish, but again, it's not as easy as just sticking your line in water and waiting for the fish to bite. If you have a rod and reel, use these tips to catch a fish:

Choose a lure that matches the color of the water. Your lure should also look as much like a fish's prey as possible.

Choose a rod. There's no one-size-fits-all fishing rod. For instance, bass fish require heavier rods, while black crappie tend to go after lighter lines and jigs. Know what fish you want to catch and match your equipment accordingly. You can always ask store clerks at bait shops for help as they are often avid fishermen themselves.

Fish early in the morning or at dusk when many fish species are most active. If you must fish during the day, try to find a shady spot that mimics the low light.

Cast your line. Once you've found a good spot, cast your line out into the water. Make sure you have enough line out to reach the bottom if you're fishing in deep water.

Be patient. Fishing requires patience. Wait for the fish to bite, and avoid making sudden movements or loud noises that could scare them away.

Set the hook. When you feel a tug on your line, quickly jerk your rod up to set the hook in the fish's mouth. Reel in the line slowly and steadily to avoid losing the fish.

Land the fish. Once you've reeled in the fish, use a net or your hands to carefully bring it out of the water. Remove the hook carefully, making sure not to injure the fish, and release it back into the water if it's not the species or size you're targeting. You can also keep it if it's within legal limits and you plan to consume it.

Clean and prepare the fish as soon as possible by scaling it and removing the guts. Rinse the fish in clean water and store it on ice until you're ready to cook it.

It's important to always follow local fishing regulations and guidelines, including bag and size limits and catch-and-release practices for certain species. Remember to respect the environment and the fish you're catching, and leave the area cleaner than you found it.

SHOOT STRAIGHT

Whether you're hunting or defending yourself, without the ability to shoot straight, you'll likely miss your target. While there are multiple factors that can affect the trajectory of a bullet (like wind and motion), you can learn to shoot a gun accurately with practice and proper technique. Here are some basic steps to follow when shooting a gun:

Get in the proper stance by standing with your feet shoulder-width apart and perpendicular to the target. Keep your weight balanced evenly on both feet, and slightly bend your knees.

Hold the gun properly by gripping it with your dominant hand and wrapping your fingers around the handle. Place your thumb on the opposite side of the gun. Place your other hand underneath the gun to help support it. Make sure your grip is firm but not too tight.

Look through the sights of the gun and align the front and rear sights with the target. The front sight should be centered in the rear sight, and the top of the front sight should be level with the top of the rear sight.

Control your breathing. Take a deep breath and exhale slowly, holding your breath just before you pull the trigger. This will help steady your aim and minimize any movement in your body.

Squeeze the trigger with the pad of your index finger. Move slowly and steadily without jerking or flinching. This will help you maintain your aim and shoot more accurately.

Follow through. After firing the gun, continue to hold it steady and keep your eyes on the target for a moment. This will help you evaluate your shot and make any necessary adjustments for the next one.

Practice regularly at a shooting range or another safe location. Gradually increase the distance between you and the target to challenge yourself and improve your skills.

IDENTIFY POISONOUS PLANTS

Nothing will ruin a camping trip or romantic hike in the woods like a rash from a poisonous plant. This is why anyone who spends time outdoors should be able to identify the six most common plants that are poisonous to humans.

The old adage "leaves of three, let them be" is a good guide for identifying poison ivy and poison oak, but poisonous plants can have as many as 10 leaves, so it's not a fail-proof method for identifying plants to avoid.

Poison sumac, which is the third-most prevalent poisonous plant, has a red stem and between 7 and 10 leaves. In the spring and summer, this plant will have small green berries that aren't perfectly round. In the fall, the berries will be white.

Giant hogweed, which contains a poisonous sap, has white, flat-topped flowers that grow in clusters at the top of the stem. The stems are thick, hairy, and green with purple splotches.

Poison hemlock is challenging to identify because it looks similar to nontoxic plants. It has lacy, fern-like leaves and clusters of white flowers that form an umbrella shape over the stem. The stem is green and ribbed with purple splotches. The fruit is egg shaped and may smell musty.

Castor bean seeds contain ricin, which can be fatal if consumed. Castor bean plants can grow up to 15 feet tall and have star-shaped leaves that are bronze or red before they reach full maturity. They have round, feathery, red flowers that grow in clusters at the top of the stem.

PICK A LOCK

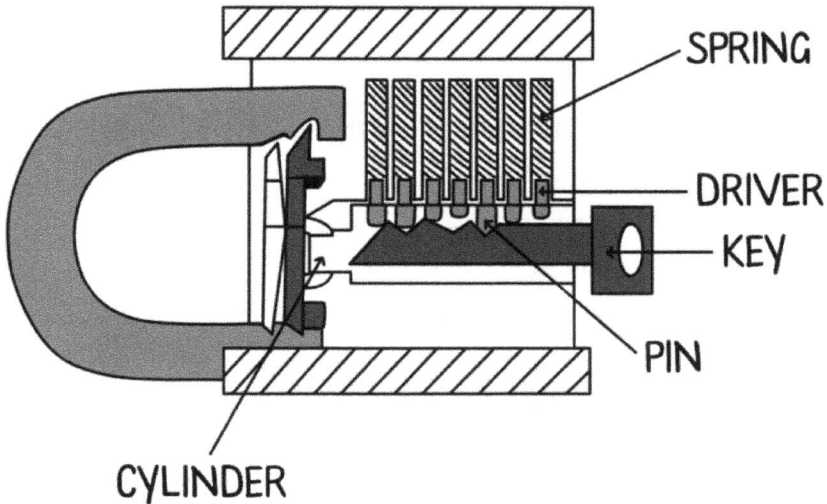

Now, we certainly aren't advocating picking locks that don't belong to you, but if you've lost the key to a lock or purchased something that's locked and didn't come with the key, knowing how to pick a lock is a good skill to have.

Picking a tumbler lock is like solving a puzzle. After all, you're just moving parts around inside the lock until they fall into place. You will need to practice on various locks to hone your skills, but here are the basic steps:

> **Gather your supplies**, which should include tension wrenches, picks, raking tools, and lock lubricant; if you don't have a professional lock-picking kit, use a bobby pin or a paperclip. *Note: It's not illegal to own a lock-picking kit unless you're using it for nefarious purposes.*

> **Picture the inside of a lock** in your mind to understand what you need to move with the picking tools to get it to open.

> **The number of pins a lock has varies** by style; in Europe, the pins are at the bottom of the keyway instead of at the top as pictured.

> **Lubricate the lock** with a spray lubricant to loosen up the insides of the mechanism.

> **Determine which way the key turns** by inserting the tension wrench inside the keyway and gently turning it. The plug will turn more easily one way or the other, which tells you which direction the key turns.

> **Use a pick** to find the pins and determine how many there are.

> **Apply light** but increasingly firm pressure on one pin to see how much force is required to lift it.

Use the tension wrench to identify the binding pin. This is the pin that causes the lock to freeze and keeps the plug from turning.

Keep steady pressure on the wrench as you set the binding pin by lifting it up. Too much pressure will freeze the lock, but too little pressure will reset the pins.

Set the rest of the pins one at a time until they are all set. You'll know when each pin sets because the tension wrench will turn the plug slightly.

If the lock freezes, you'll have to release the tension on your wrench to allow the pins to reset so that you can start over.

PILOT A BOAT

There is no one way to pilot a boat as it depends on what type of boat you're in, but you'll be able to understand the basics with these tips:

If the boat uses gasoline and has an engine compartment, use the blower (exhaust fan) to ensure there hasn't been a buildup of fumes.

Remove all lines securing the boat to the dock, slip, or pier. Raise the anchor.

Put the key in the ignition and turn it or push the start button if it's a modern boat.

Many boats have a kill switch that automatically turns off the boat if you leave the helm. If the boat you're driving has a kill switch, attach the lanyard to a clip on your life jacket.

Check that all your passengers are ready to depart.

Gently push the throttle away from you to move forward, or pull backward to move in reverse.

When the boat is in motion, turn the wheel just as you would in a motor vehicle to determine the direction of travel.

Trim the boat as necessary for the weather conditions. In other words, adjust the *attitude* of the boat. The attitude is the angle at which the bow meets the water.

To slow down, gently move the throttle back toward the neutral position in the middle.

It's a good idea to practice these skills in advance, but if for some reason you need to step in to pilot a boat for a friend or in an emergency, these steps should get you to where you need to go.

ALWAYS KNOW NORTH

As mentioned in the navigation section, always carrying a compass is the easiest way to always know where north is, but there are several ways to determine north without a compass. You'll have to practice each one of them to truly master this skill.

If it's night, identify the North Star. If you're in the northern hemisphere, the North Star is fairly easy to find. While it's not the brightest star in the night sky, it is fairly prominent and can be found relatively quickly if you can locate the Big Dipper constellation. Find the two stars at the blade end of the big dipper, then draw an imaginary line through these two stars. Follow the line upward until you reach the North Star.

If it's night and you can't find the North Star, find two sticks, one slightly longer than the other, and lie down on your stomach. Push the shorter stick into the ground until it's at eye level. Take the longer stick and push it into the ground in front of the first one, lining it up with a bright star from your position. Wait ten minutes and check it again. If the star moves to your left, you're facing north. If it moves to your right, you're facing south. It if moves up, you're facing east, and if it moves down, you're facing west.

Look for moss. Moss can only grow in damp conditions, which means it typically grows on the north side of land features where it's always shady. To avoid being misled by moss growing in standing water, look for moss that is growing on a vertical structure such as a tree or the side of a building.

REVERSE HYPOTHERMIA

Hypothermia, which is the condition of having abnormally low body temperature, is a potentially fatal situation that arises from being exposed to dangerously cold temperatures for an extended period of time. Signs of hypothermia include shivering, confusion, fumbling hands, drowsiness, and slurred speech. In children, hypothermia is characterized by cold, bright-red skin and lethargy.

A person doesn't even have to be outside to get hypothermia. They can be in an extremely cold room (especially babies and the elderly) or be stranded in a car in cold temperatures. Reversing hypothermia is critical to a victim's survival. The key to reversing hypothermia is to increase the victim's core body temperature in any way possible.

Remove wet clothing from anyone who's coming in from rain or snow with signs of hypothermia.

A victim who has mild hypothermia can be warmed up by covering them with an electric blanket and/or providing them with a warm beverage to drink.

If you don't have an electric blanket to warm the person, get them under loose blankets, clothing, towels, or sheets. Use skin-to-skin contact to warm them up.

Do not give the victim alcohol. If the person is unconscious, don't attempt to give them any fluids at all.

Once the victim's body temperature is increased, dress them in dry clothes and cover them with a blanket, preferably an electric blanket.

Get medical assistance for the victim as soon as possible.

If the victim is unconscious and not breathing, perform CPR on them, even if you think they might be dead. In some cases, people who have apparently died have been successfully revived because their heart rate had slowed tremendously due to the cold.

PERFORM
THE HEIMLICH

The Heimlich maneuver is intended to dislodge a piece of food or other object that has become stuck in someone's airway, preventing them from breathing. The procedure is slightly different for children than for adults, but the goal is the same: to use forced air to dislodge the object from the airway and prevent the victim from choking to death.

If a person is coughing, they are still getting air into their lungs. Don't perform the Heimlich maneuver on someone who is still able to draw air into their lungs, even if they are coughing.

If a person is not coughing, can't talk, and is turning blue or gray, stand to the side of a choking adult or kneel at the side of a choking child.

Place your arm across the victim's chest to support their body.

Bend the victim over at the waist so that they're facing the ground.

Using the heel of your hand, strike the victim in the back five times between their shoulder blades.

If the object is not expelled with back blows, move behind the person and make a fist with one hand, placing the thumb side of your fist just above the person's navel but below the rib cage. Grasp your fist with your other hand and press into the person's abdomen with a quick, upward thrust. Perform five abdominal thrusts. Use slightly less pressure on a child to avoid damaging internal organs.

Alternate five back blows with five abdominal thrusts until the object is dislodged or assistance arrives.

TIE A KNOT

There are too many types of knots to teach here, but knowing how to tie different kinds of knots for their respective purposes is a useful skill no matter what you end up doing in life. Whether you need to tie knots for your profession (e.g., a necktie knot) or for recreation (e.g., a square or bowline knot), knowing how to tie different knots will give you options in various situations.

Square knots should only be used to secure non-essential items such as packages and shoelaces because they can come loose very easily. Never use a square knot for climbing or securing two ropes together. Square knots can also be used for first aid procedures such as tying a tourniquet around a bleeding wound or fitting a sling around a person's neck.

- Take the ends of two ropes and lay them side by side with one end on the left and the other on the right.
- Cross the rope on the left over the rope on the right to make a loop.
- Bring the rope on the right up and over the loop, then pass it through the loop.
- Hold the ends of both ropes and pull them tight to create the first half of the square knot.
- To complete the knot, take the rope that is now on the left and cross it over the rope that is now on the right to make a new loop.
- Bring the rope on the right up and over the new loop, then pass it through the loop.
- Hold the ends of both ropes and pull them tight to complete the square knot.

The finished knot should look like two interlocking loops that lie flat against each other. Make sure that the knot is tight and secure before using it.

Use a **bowline knot** for emergency situations out in the wilderness. This knot is also called a rescue knot because it is used by rescue professionals to pull victims out of fire, water, or off a mountain.

- Make a small loop in the rope with the tail end of the rope on the bottom and the working end of the rope on the top.
- Bring the working end of the rope up through the loop from underneath.
- Wrap the working end of the rope around the standing end of the rope, starting from the back and wrapping around to the front.
- Bring the working end of the rope back down through the loop from the top.
- Hold the standing end of the rope with one hand and the working end with the other hand and pull them in opposite directions to tighten the knot.

The finished knot should form a loop that will not slip or come undone under load. To untie the knot, simply pull on the tail end of the rope to loosen the loop.

Sheet bends are meant for tying two ropes of different materials together. The loop of one rope is tied around the loop of the second rope. This knot won't move even if the ropes are tugged on from either end.

- Form a loop at the end of the thicker rope with the tail end of the loop on the bottom and the working end of the rope on the top.

- Pass the working end of the thinner rope through the loop from underneath.
- Wrap the working end of the thinner rope around the standing end of the thicker rope, then bring it back down through the loop.
- Hold the standing end of the thicker rope with one hand and the working end of the thinner rope with the other hand and pull them in opposite directions to tighten the knot.

The finished knot should look like a loop formed by the thicker rope with the thinner rope wrapped around it and tucked back through the loop. To untie the knot, simply pull on the working end of the thinner rope and the knot will come undone.

Two half-hitch knots are used to tie a rope to a post, tree, or ring. They're valuable for situations like tying a boat to a dock because the knot can be loosened or tightened depending on the need.

- Wrap the working end of the rope around the post or object, passing the end over the standing part of the rope.
- Bring the working end of the rope over the standing part again, then tuck it underneath and back over itself to create a loop.
- Pass the working end of the rope through the loop from the bottom, pulling it tight to create the first half-hitch knot.
- Repeat the process by creating a second half-hitch knot, passing the working end of the rope over the standing part, creating another loop, and passing the working end through the loop from the bottom.

The finished knots should look like two loops around the post with the working end of the rope passing through both loops. To untie

34

the knots, simply pull on the working end of the rope to release each half-hitch knot in turn.

Taut-line hitches are great for ropes that need to be pulled tight, like those securing a tent to the ground. They can be loosened or tightened easily by pushing the knot up or down the tightened part of the rope.

- Wrap the working end of the rope around a fixed object, passing it over and then underneath the standing part of the rope to create a loop.
- Bring the working end of the rope back up through the loop from underneath, then wrap it around the standing part of the rope twice.
- Bring the working end of the rope back down through the loop again, passing it under the standing part of the rope.
- Hold the standing part of the rope with one hand and the working end of the rope with the other hand and pull them in opposite directions to tighten the knot.
- To adjust the tension, hold the knot with one hand and use the other hand to slide the loops up or down the standing part of the rope as needed.

The finished knot should look like a loop around the fixed object with the working end of the rope wrapped around the standing part of the rope and passing through the loop twice. The knot should be adjustable to allow for changes in tension as needed. To untie the knot, simply reverse the steps, sliding the loops down and removing the working end of the rope from the knot.

DEVELOP A
CLEANING ROUTINE

Cleaning properly isn't hard if you manage upkeep regularly. The trick is to create a daily routine that keeps you in the habit of picking up so that deep cleans take less time. Deep cleaning should take place at least twice a year.

Daily chores include:

- Making your bed
- Cleaning your dishes/coffee pot
- Wiping down kitchen and bathroom counters
- Knocking out full loads of laundry
- Sweeping floors, especially the kitchen

Weekly chores include:

- Deep cleaning/sanitizing bathrooms
- Wiping down mirrors
- Vacuuming
- Mopping
- Dusting
- Washing/changing bedding
- Cleaning out expired food from the fridge
- Cleaning microwave

Once monthly chores include:

- Cleaning the refrigerator
- Cleaning the oven
- Cleaning the dishwasher

- Cleaning out dryer vents
- Cleaning your vehicle (inside and out)

On a semi-annual basis, you should:

- Clean behind hard-to-reach places like the refrigerator and stove
- Clean under heavy furniture
- Clean under the bed
- Wash windows
- Wash walls
- Wash window coverings
- Clean gutters

Knowing how to clean and knowing how to clean *properly* are two different things. Most people can figure out how to use a duster or a broom, but they might not be cleaning very well at all. These tips can help:

- Choose one chore at a time and complete that chore throughout the entire house.
- Keep all your cleaning supplies together in a portable caddy.
- Before you start cleaning, clear the clutter in every room.
- Dust first (don't forget the ceiling fans), then sweep/vacuum.
- Clean and disinfect high-contact surfaces (e.g., doorknobs, countertops, appliances, cabinets, doors, light switches, television remotes, telephones, etc.)

- Spray cleaner on bathroom surfaces like the toilet, sink, and shower and allow it to sit for a few minutes before scrubbing.

- Clean toilets last.

- Sweep first, then mop.

- Keep your cleaning tools clean. This is something a lot of people forget to do, but an unclean tool isn't cleaning anything.

TAKE CARE OF A FANCY PLANT

Some people have green thumbs and every plant under their care thrives. Other people, well, *don't*. If it seems like every plant you've ever tried to care for has died, don't give up. Live plants perform many beneficial tasks in your home including reducing stress levels, eliminating air pollutants, and boosting your mood, among others.

The key to keeping a plant alive is choosing the right plant for your environment and lifestyle. There are some plants that are simply too hard to care for, but there are also some that can thrive with minimal effort on your part. There are many hard-to-kill plants to choose from, including the following:

- Hoya (wax plant)

- Rubber plant (ficus)

- Snake plant

- Spider plant

- Aloe vera
- Madagascar dragon tree
- Chinese evergreen
- Jade plant
- Zebra haworthia
- Ponytail palm
- ZZ plant
- Umbrella tree
- Cast iron plant
- Peace lily
- Hindu rope plant
- Purple shamrock
- Parlor palm
- Philodendrons
- Orchid
- Various cactus species

Choosing one or several of these plants will enhance your home and make it feel more inviting. No matter which plant or plants you have in your house, follow these tips to keep them healthy:

- Water them on an as-needed basis rather than a set schedule. Each plant requires a different amount of water, so pay attention to recommendations from professional gardeners.
- Fertilize your plants according to the label or find online instructions for the species you're caring for.

- Propagate plants (start new plants from existing ones) to encourage fresh growth.

- Repot overgrown plants into larger pots. Check the root system to determine if your plant has outgrown its pot. If the roots are circling the container, the plant may need a larger space.

- Gently remove dust from the leaves with a cloth.

- Prune your plants in the fall (or more often for fast-growing plants) to encourage growth.

- Remove dying leaves.

- Use an insecticide to prevent household pests. This is usually a spray treatment.

IRON CLOTHES

While ironing clothes isn't as fashionable as it used to be when most materials wrinkled if you breathed on them, it's still important to have freshly pressed clothing when you want to make a good impression. It's particularly important for men who often wear suits and dress shirts as those items don't look good with wrinkles.

The action of ironing is not all that difficult, but you do have to be careful not to burn your clothes. Follow these steps to get crisply ironed clothing every time:

- Wash your clothes first. Ironing dirty clothes is just a waste of time.

- Use an ironing board. While you can use any solid surface in your home as a base for ironing, it isn't recommended because the heat from the iron can damage those surfaces. Get an ironing board that you can fold up and store behind a door or in a closet.

- Check the labels on your clothing for ironing instructions. Some materials are extremely sensitive to heat, so pay attention to the recommended temperatures for your articles.

- Preheat the iron to the recommended temperature or setting based on the label's instructions.

- Turn the article of clothing inside out, and lay it flat on the ironing board. Ironing the inside of the item gets the wrinkles out without damaging more delicate materials like silk and linen.

- Spray the article of clothing with water to dampen it. Wrinkles come out better if the material is damp (not soaked).

- Press the iron gently on the material, moving it around frequently. Don't allow the iron to sit in any one spot for long as this is a major cause of burns. It can also lead to a fire if you leave it too long.

- Iron each element of the article of clothing separately. For example, lay each sleeve flat, then move the shirt to lay the collar flat, etc.

- Turn the iron off and allow it to cool before storing it. This should only take about 10 minutes.

- Hang your newly ironed clothing on a hanger to prevent it from getting wrinkled again before you wear it.

WET SHAVE

The wet shave is the most common type of shave because it delivers the best results. With that said, it's easy to damage your skin while trying to get a close shave, especially if you're inexperienced. Here's how to get the smoothest shave possible:

Clean your face. The perfect time to shave is right after you get out of the shower because your skin will be warm and soft. If you can't take a shower before shaving, use a wet, warm towel to soften and warm your skin.

Let your shaving brush soak. This is a key step in getting the closest wet shave. Soak it in warm water for a couple of minutes, then hold it under a stream of hot water until it starts to feel heavy. Shake the excess water off while keeping the brush still wet.

Use your shaving brush to apply shaving cream. Don't move the brush in a circular motion. Instead, flick it back and forth to work up a lather. Apply the cream in an upward motion to lift the hair and make it easier to shave.

Warm your razor under a hot tap for about 10 seconds before beginning the shaving process.

Move the razor gently across your skin in the same direction of hair growth. Moving against the grain will irritate the skin and make it more likely that you'll cut yourself.

Remember not to press too hard as this also leads to cuts and nicks. The razor is designed to glide across a flat surface, so very little pressure is actually necessary.

Fill your sink with fresh, warm water and use it to rinse your face.

Follow up the warm rinse with a cold one to close your pores.

Pat your face dry with a clean cloth. Don't rub the cloth across your face since that can irritate your skin.

Apply an after-shave balm to moisturize the skin and reduce post-shave irritation.

PACK A SUITCASE OR TRAVEL BAG

The key to properly packing a suitcase or travel bag is to ensure you have room for everything you need both going and coming back. Most travelers pack more items than they really need, so before you try to stuff your suitcase full of things that won't even come out when you arrive at your destination, take a few minutes to edit your selections, then follow these tips for packing:

Gather the items you will need while you're gone. Choose one shirt for every day you'll be away and a spare just in case anything happens. Make sure you have a matching pair of shorts or pants for each shirt.

Choose wrinkle-resistant clothing that can withstand rolling and folding.

Roll items that don't wrinkle or don't need to look nice such as underwear, socks, and pajamas. Fold stiffer items like slacks and dress shirts.

Place the rolled items at the bottom of your suitcase or on top of shoes, if you're bringing a spare pair.

Your middle layer will be your folded items. Alternate waists and hems so that the bulky waists won't all be in one place taking up more room than they should.

Place clothing you will need first at the top so that you can get to it easily without unpacking everything.

Place a plastic bag between layers to help you get to lower layers more quickly. While unpacking, just pick up the ends of the bag to remove the upper layers.

Snake belts around the edge of the bag so that they don't take up much room.

Cover the entire pile of clothing with a dry-cleaning bag to help reduce wrinkles.

If packing shoes, stuff items inside them (if the shoes are clean) to use all available space.

Choose miniature versions of your toiletries and place them in a separate bag that can fit in a gap in your suitcase.

Don't forget to bring an empty laundry or garbage bag for dirty clothes so that you can store them away from your clean clothes, even if you have to keep them both in the suitcase for the duration of your trip.

TIE A TIE

① ② ③
④ ⑤ ⑥

No matter how hard you try to avoid formal events and situations, you will probably need to wear a necktie at some point in your life.

Turn your collar up and place your necktie around your neck so that the middle of the tie is flush against the back of your collar. Make sure the seam is down.

Start with the wide end of the tie on your right side and the narrow end on your left. The wide end should be longer than the narrow end with the tip of the wide end hanging about 12 inches lower than the narrow one.

Cross the wide end of the tie over the narrow end, then bring it up and over the narrow end again.

Bring the wide end down and tuck it behind the narrow end, then bring it up and over the narrow end again.

Bring the wide end down and tuck it up behind the loop around your neck, then bring it down through the loop in front of the knot.

Hold the narrow end of the tie with one hand and the knot with the other hand and gently pull the knot up toward your neck to tighten it.

Adjust the knot as needed by pulling on the wide end of the tie and sliding the knot up or down until it's positioned where you want it.

The finished knot should look like a neat and symmetrical triangle with the narrow end of the tie tucked behind the knot. With a bit of practice, you'll be able to tie a tie quickly and easily.

SEW

Sewing may seem like an antiquated skill, but believe it or not, it's still handy to know, especially if you need to quickly repair a seam or hole or replace a button. You don't have to own a sewing machine to handle minor sewing duties, but you do need to master some basic stitches to make sure your repairs look presentable.

The running stitch is ideal for sewing patches over holes in clothing, repairing a hem, and reattaching a strap or other piece of fabric back onto the main piece. All you need for a running stitch is a needle and some thread. Thread your needle, tie a knot, and move the needle in and out of the fabric at regular intervals.

Note that the running stitch, which is the easiest of all stitches, will look the same on both sides of the fabric, so you don't have to worry about which is the "better" side.

- Thread your needle with a length of thread and tie a knot at the end.
- Starting from the back ofthe fabric, bring your needle up through the fabric at the starting point of the new seam.
- Insert the needle back down through the fabric about 1/4 inch away from the starting point, pulling the thread all the way through.
- Continue sewing in this manner, making straight stitches of equal length along the length of the intended seam.
- Keep the stitches evenly spaced and the tension of the thread consistent throughout the seam.
- To finish the seam, tie a knot at the end and clip the excess thread.

The back stitch is a variation of the running stitch, but it's stronger because you sew two running stitches, then go back over the second running stitch before moving forward by two again. This is a good choice for reattaching zippers where the seam has come apart and repairing rips or tears that are away from the seam.

- Thread your needle with a length of thread and tie a knot at the end.
- Starting from the back of the fabric, bring your needle up through the fabric at the starting point of the seam.

- Insert the needle back down through the fabric about 1/4 inch away from the starting point, pulling the thread all the way through.
- Bring the needle up through the fabric at a point about halfway between the starting point and the end of the first stitch.
- Insert the needle back down through the fabric at the end of the first stitch, making sure to pass the needle through the loop of the previous stitch.
- Bring the needle up through the fabric at a point about halfway between the end of the first stitch and the end of the second stitch.
- Insert the needle back down through the fabric at the end of the second stitch, passing the needle through the loop of the previous stitch.
- Continue sewing in this manner, making even stitches of equal length along the length of the intended seam.
- Keep the stitches evenly spaced and the tension of the thread consistent throughout the seam.
- To finish the seam, tie a knot at the end and clip the excess thread.

Of the three basic stitches, the whip stitch is the most complicated. If you have a situation like a busted seam, a split-open pocket, or a hem that has split open away from the seam, it's the best option for repair. Choose a thread that matches your fabric for this one because it will show on the outside of the material. This stitch is basically the running stitch but on a diagonal.

- Thread your needle with a length of thread and tie a knot at the end.
- Align the edges of the two pieces of fabric you want to join together.

- Starting at one end of the fabric, bring your needle up through the bottom layer of fabric near the edge.
- Insert the needle back down through both layers of fabric, about 1/4 inch away from the starting point.
- Bring the needle up through the bottom layer of fabric again, this time close to where the thread exited the fabric in the first step.
- Insert the needle back down through both layers of fabric, close to where the thread entered in the previous step.
- Repeat steps 5 and 6, making stitches that are about 1/4 inch in length, until you reach the end of the fabric.
- To finish the stitch, tie a knot at the end and clip the excess thread.

Sewing on a button is essentially combining a running stitch through the holes of the button, either in a straight line (for a two-hole button) or a crossing pattern (for a four-hole button).

- Place the button on the fabric and push the needle through the fabric and one of the holes.
- Turn the needle and push it through the opposite hole and back down through the fabric.
- It's very important to avoid pulling the threads too tightly as you want to leave space for the fabric to fit nicely underneath once buttoned. Pull the thread all the way to the end each time you go through the hole.
- Repeat these steps for as many times as it takes to ensure the button is securely fastened to the material. Tie off the thread at the back of the material.

SHINE SHOES

Clean shoes say a lot about how much you care about yourself and your appearance. When you go to an interview or out on a date, people really do pay attention to your entire ensemble. Purchasing good shoes that are made from high-quality materials is the first step toward keeping your shoes nice, but you should also know how to shine them so that you leave a great impression wherever you go.

Gather your shoe-shining supplies. You will need a shoe brush that is designed specifically for shining shoes or a soft-bristled toothbrush; shoe polish in cream, wax, or liquid form; and a shoe buffer, which is a soft cloth that you'll attach to a drill. You may also want a few Q-tips on hand.

If your shoes are particularly dirty, you may need shoe cleaner.

If you use wax or cream polish, you will also need a polishing cloth.

Remove the laces from your shoes.

Stuff your shoes with paper to give yourself a firm surface to polish.

Remove dirt and debris by wetting your shoe brush or toothbrush and brushing your shoe in a circular motion to loosen the dirt.

If your shoes have a lot of dirt, use the shoe cleaner to remove as much as possible. Follow the directions on the shoe cleaner to get the best results.

Once all dirt is removed, move on to the polishing step. If even a particle of dirt is left, it could scratch the leather, so it's crucial to get your shoes as clean as possible.

Apply a thin layer of polish to your shoes and rub it into the leather using a circular motion.

Allow the polish to sit for several minutes and absorb into the leather.

Use a Q-tip to rub the polish into hard-to-reach places.

Once the polish is dry, apply a thin second layer of polish in the same manner as the first.

Apply as many layers of polish as necessary to coat the entire shoe. It's better to apply several thin layers of polish than one thick layer.

After the last layer of polish is dry, attach the shoe buffer to your drill and turn it on the lowest setting.

Hold the buffer against the shoe and move in a circular motion until your shoe is shiny.

Use the shoe brush to remove any excess shoe polish. Remember to brush in a circular motion.

Dry your shoes and lace them.

Shine your shoes every month to six weeks for best results.

UNCLOG A TOILET

There are some DIY repairs that should be left to professionals, but unclogging a toilet isn't one of them. You can save a lot of money by learning how to get your toilet unclogged without calling a plumber. There are several DIY ways to unclog a toilet, but the most common is by using a plunger, which you should keep by every toilet in the house.

Insert the plunger into the toilet bowl.

If there isn't enough water in the toilet bowl to **cover the base of the plunger** (the rubber part), pour some sink water in the toilet bowl until the water covers the base.

The plunger must be fully submerged in water so that you're creating suction with water and not air.

Fully cover the hole in the toilet that leads to the drain with the base of the plunger.

Pump the plunger over the hole. Be sure to pump gently at first because the initial pump will draw in air and could cause the water to splash.

Continue pushing and pulling on the plunger, keeping the base of the plunger fully submerged until the water starts to drain.

You may have to push and pull on the plunger up to 20 times before a stubborn clog comes loose.

When you believe you have removed the clog, flush the toilet to check that it drains properly.

Flush the toilet several more times to make sure the clog has moved out of your sewer lines.

GARDEN

Believe it or not, gardening used to be mostly a man's activity, especially when the world relied primarily on agriculture for survival. You never know when you might need to know how to grow a garden for those purposes again; plus, it's just nice to know that you can feed yourself if you really have to.

There are many complex gardening skills to learn if you want to become an advanced gardener, but there are also plenty of basic gardening skills that can get you started.

Soil preparation:

Several types of soil exist if you're starting a garden from scratch. Either purchase top soil, compost, or peat moss, or use the natural soil in your own yard.

If you choose your own dirt, till it by hand or with a rototiller that you can rent from an equipment rental store.

Analyze your soil using a store-bought kit to see which nutrients it's missing.

Add fertilizer that contains the nutrients your soil is missing.

Keep working year after year to improve your soil by adding compost, top soil, and other components as needed.

Water:

Newly planted seeds require steady moisture but not heavy water. Keep the soil moist but not drenched.

Once the plants have sprouted, water once or twice a week. Overwatering leads to a shallow root system, which means you'll have to water even more. Give your plants enough water to saturate six inches of soil.

If the temperatures are extremely hot or there has been an extended drought, water them a little more often.

Sunlight:

Choose a location for your garden that will give your plants six to eight hours of sunlight per day.

Choose plants that grow better in the sunlight conditions you have. For example, lettuces, cauliflower, kale, spinach, carrots, beets, peas, and parsley, among others, grow better in partial sun of 4–6 hours per day. Beans, cabbage, squash, cucumbers, corn, melons, peppers, and tomatoes grow better in full sun of greater than 6 hours per day.

Garden care:

Weeding your garden is necessary, but if you plant your garden thickly, the plants themselves will create a canopy that helps keep weeds to a minimum.

Adding a layer of mulch like dead grass or leaves discourages the growth of weeds.

Pull weeds when they are small so that they don't take over your garden. This means you should weed for 15–20 minutes daily.

Timing:

Knowing when to plant certain vegetables and when to harvest them is key to a successful garden.

Read the instructions on your seeds to know when the best time to plant them is and when they will reach full maturity.

SHARPEN A KNIFE

Whether it's a hunting knife or a steak knife, if it's dull, it won't work the way it should. In fact, a dull knife can be even more of a safety hazard than a sharp one. With a dull knife, you'll have to work harder to cut through the material, which can lead to reckless use of the blade. Of course, using an electric knife sharpener is the easiest way to sharpen a knife, but if you don't have one of those handy, follow these steps:

Use a whetstone that's specifically designed for sharpening knives.

If you don't have a whetstone, choose a smooth, flat stone that's been in or along a river (if possible).

Place the whetstone on a non-slip surface. If you're sharpening your knife on a countertop, place a towel underneath the stone for traction.

Some whetstones need to be wetted before use, so follow the directions that came with your whetstone before starting.

Make sure the coarser side of the whetstone is facing up.

Hold the knife against the whetstone surface so that the edge of the blade is facing you at a 15- or 20-degree angle.

Rest the fingers of your other hand on the flat side of the knife and push the knife away from you in one stroke.

Repeat this motion 10–20 times or until the knife is sharp.

Test the sharpness with paper or a tomato.

SAFELY SET UP
AN EXTENSION LADDER

Every year, more than 100 people in the U.S. die and thousands more are injured from ladder accidents. There are so many ladder-related incidents that the entire month of March is actually dedicated to ladder safety! To keep yourself from becoming a statistic, you need to learn how to safely set up an extension ladder on an exterior wall.

Both feet of the ladder should be on level ground. If necessary, dig a small hole to ensure both feet are even.

The feet of the ladder should be on solid, dry ground. They should not be set on wet ground where they can sink in or on slippery surfaces like tarps or debris.

If the ground is soft, tie 1-inch by 2-inch stakes to the sides of each foot and drive them into the ground.

Position the ladder at a 75-degree angle so that the distance between the wall and the ladder is one quarter of the ladder's height at its resting point.

When you stand facing the ladder with your feet touching its feet, your palms should rest on a rung that is at shoulder height.

Always check for overhead wires before setting up or climbing a ladder.

Don't position the ladder too close to the edge of a roof.

If necessary, use a ladder stabilizer to extend away from the wall a few inches to give yourself more room to work.

Ladder jacks should only be used on ladders up to 20 feet. Any higher than that, and you need a harness.

Always keep the tread clean and clear from tools and debris.

PAINT A ROOM

Whether you're a homeowner or not, you'll likely paint a room or two in your life, and there's more to it than just slapping a new coat of paint on the walls and calling it good. Even if you want it done quickly, there's still a right way and a wrong way to paint a room. These tips show you how to do it right:

Clean the walls. It's tempting to skip this step, but even if they don't look dirty, *your walls are dirty*. They have accumulated small particles of dust and grime that make it harder for the paint to stick. Use mild dishwashing soap, water, and a cellulose sponge to clean your walls, then rinse them with water to remove any soap residue. Allow the walls to fully dry.

Fill nail holes with spackle and lightly sand to create a smooth surface.

Use blue painter's tape to mark off trim, window frames, and door frames. This tape can be applied up to a week ahead of time.

Prime the walls, even if they've been painted before. A fresh coat of primer keeps the previous color from showing through and maximizes the coverage of the new paint.

Use a two-inch angled paintbrush to paint around the trim and in corners before rolling paint on the walls. This helps prevent brush strokes around the edges. Many people cut in after they've rolled on the paint, but this makes the edges obvious, whereas doing it first allows you to hide the edges under the rolled paint.

Use a W pattern to roll the paint on the walls. Start in one corner and make a three-by-three-foot W pattern with the paint. Then fill in the W without lifting the roller. Repeat this pattern in sections until the entire wall is painted. For the most uniform coverage, paint one wall at a time.

When the walls are completely dry, tape where the trim meets the wall and paint the trim.

CRAFT A COCKTAIL OR TWO

Sure, you can always mix a rum and coke for your friends, but that doesn't take much effort, and you can really impress your guests by knowing how to craft a basic cocktail or two. Keep the ingredients for these cocktails on hand and you'll always have a go-to drink in case someone drops by.

Martini: Add two parts gin or vodka with one part vermouth in a glass with ice and stir. Strain into a chilled martini glass. Add an olive or twist of lemon for garnish.

Negroni: Mix together equal parts gin, Campari, and sweet vermouth in a glass filled with ice. Let sit until chilled, then strain into a new glass with fresh ice or a chilled glass without ice for a straight-up Negroni.

Old fashioned: Mix together two ounces of bourbon or rye whiskey, 2–3 dashes of Angostura bitters, and one sugar cube (or 1 teaspoon of sugar). Add a couple of large ice cubes and stir rapidly. Strain into a fresh glass with ice. Add a slice of orange or a cherry for garnish.

Manhattan: Mix together four ounces of rye whiskey, two ounces of sweet vermouth, and four dashes of Angostura bitters. Pour over ice and shake until the shaker is cold to the touch. Add a maraschino cherry for garnish.

Margarita: Run a slice of lime around the edge of a glass and dip the glass in rock salt. In a cocktail shaker, mix four ounces of white tequila, two ounces of triple sec, one and a half ounces of fresh lime juice, and ice. Shake until chilled. Pour into fresh glass filled with ice, and garnish with a lime wheel.

STAY FIT

As you're likely already aware, physical health is a major key to living a long life. While there's no guarantee that you won't experience medical issues as you age, being physically fit gives you the best chance to avoid them.

According to the Centers for Disease Control (CDC), an adult needs a minimum of 150 minutes of exercise each week, which averages out to 30 minutes per workday. The CDC also recommends performing strength activities such as weightlifting two times per week. These muscle-building activities should target all major muscle groups (e.g., arms, legs, hips, back, abdomen, and chest).

It's not necessary to complete all 30 minutes of exercise at one time. You can break them up in three 10-minute sessions or two 15-minute sessions if it fits your schedule better. Or, if you don't want to exercise five days a week, you can choose longer sessions for fewer days. What matters is that you move for a minimum of 150 total minutes each week.

If you're starting from scratch, it's always recommended that you talk to your doctor before beginning any kind of exercise regimen. This ensures your body is healthy enough to perform the types of exercise at the intensity you need to stay fit.

Of course, eating right is also a part of health. The more vegetables and fruits you eat, the better your diet is, but there's no reason you can't have other foods in moderation as well. The CDC recommends that you eat the following on a daily basis:

- Two and a half servings of vegetables, which can be canned, frozen, fresh, or dried

- Two servings of fruit, which can be canned, frozen, fresh, or dried

- Six servings of whole grains (not refined)

- Three servings of low-fat or fat-free dairy

- Five and a half ounces of lean proteins such as legumes, nuts, fish, seafood, skinless poultry, or lean beef. Avoid processed meats. Limit nuts to five ounces per week and seafood to six to eight ounces per week.

- Three tablespoons of healthy fats (e.g., canola, corn, olive, soybean, or safflower oil)

GRILL WITH CHARCOAL

Almost anyone can grill on a propane grill, but it takes more effort and skill to grill with charcoal. This is not only the oldest form of grilling, but it also arguably produces the tastiest results. The hardest part about grilling with charcoal is getting the charcoal lit, and while it's tempting to use lighter fluid to make it easier, it's better not to use any accelerant at all to avoid affecting the taste of the food.

These tips for lighting a charcoal grill and grilling with charcoal will make you the king of the backyard barbecue:

- **Use a charcoal chimney to start your charcoal grill.** Pack the base of the chimney with crumpled paper and place the charcoal on top.

- **Light the bottom of the chimney** where the paper is and wait 15–20 minutes for the charcoal to heat up.

- **You will know the charcoal is ready** when it turns white with ash and begins to glow.

- **The higher the temperature**, the more charcoal you'll need to use. For example, if you're cooking a steak over high heat, fill the charcoal chimney completely full. If you're cooking something more delicate like fish or chicken, the chimney only needs to be half full. For pork or brisket, which you want to cook slowly over low heat, only fill a quarter of the chimney.

- **Add hickory, mesquite, walnut, or cherry wood** to enhance the flavor of your food, especially if you're cooking brisket, pork, or ribs.

- **Use the vents** on your charcoal grill to control the heat.

- **Ensure your charcoals are fully extinguished** by closing the vents to cut off oxygen.

- **You can reuse partially burned charcoal** briquets the next time you grill.

PROPERLY POUR BEER

An improperly poured beer can actually cause a stomachache. This is because beer that's poured to get as little foam as possible contains trapped CO_2 that expands in your stomach. You want that carbonation to expand in the glass and not in your body, so pouring a beer correctly is important.

Hold your glass at a 45-degree angle from the beer or beer tap.

Line up the opening of the bottle, can, or tap at the side of the glass near the middle.

Pour the beer, leaving a little room between the edge of the glass and the bottle, can, or tap.

Once your glass is about halfway full, straighten it up and pour the rest of the beer into the glass.

Your beer should have a foamy head, which is all that released carbonation releasing in your glass instead of in your stomach.

COOK EVERY
TYPE OF STEAK

Each cut of steak requires a slightly different cooking technique; you can actually ruin a good piece of meat by preparing it incorrectly. For this reason, men should know how to identify the type of steak they have and how to cook it properly for the best flavor.

Rump:

- Rump steak is a lean cut of meat that comes from the rear of the animal, so there won't be as much marbling.

- The ideal size of a rump steak is two inches thick.

- Since it's a muscular cut, it requires a minimum of three minutes of cooking on each side and lots of basting. The heat and moisture are necessary to break down the fibrous meat and make it tender enough to eat.

- Allow this steak to rest for at least 10 minutes after cooking.

Ribeye:

- Ribeye steak comes from ribs six through twelve on a cow.

- It should be well marbled with a central layer of fat running through the steak.

- This steak has a lot of fat, so it can be eaten rare.

- Heat your pan on the stove's highest setting and wait an additional 30 seconds before adding the meat.

- Sear the steak until it's the color and temperature you like.

Sirloin:

- You'll find sirloin steaks at the middle back of a cow covering the spine.

- Many of these steaks are aged up to 60 days and will be dark red.

- Sirloin steaks require fat rendering, so heat your pan up to high.

- Cook the steak until the fat on the entire steak turns golden brown.

- Sirloin can be eaten rare, medium, or well done, but it needs to rest for the same amount of time it was cooked.

Fillet or filet mignon:

- Fillet steaks are found inside the sirloin along the side of a cow's spine.

- This is the leanest meat of a cow and often the most expensive cut.

- Look for a thick cut of similar width so that it cooks evenly.

- Cook fillet steaks over medium heat until they are rare or medium rare.

- Baste often to break down the fibrous muscle, and be careful not to overcook or the meat will be too tough to eat.

T-Bone:

- This steak is part sirloin and part fillet and is found on the lower middle of the cow. It has a T-shaped bone that divides the two types of steaks.

- Make sure your T-bone has a nice portion of both types of steaks.

- Since the two types require different cooking times, this cut can be tricky. Sear the entire steak with the bone in over high heat, then transfer it to a 200-degree oven until it reaches the desired internal temperature and is tender enough to eat.

Flank:

- Flank steak is found just above the cow's kidney and liver on the end of the inner flank.

- Despite being one of the least expensive steaks, it can also be one of the most flavorful if prepared properly.

- Tenderize the flank steak, which should be flat and fairly thin, by marinating it overnight. A simple marinade of olive oil, soy sauce, lime juice, coriander, and salt will make the steak taste fabulous the next day. Keep it in a bag in the fridge overnight, then bring up to room temperature before searing for four minutes on each side.

Hanger:

- This cut of meat is found next to the cow's diaphragm and runs through the middle of the animal.

- The flavor of hanger meat is a little gamier than other cuts because it's near the vital organs.

- Hanger meat should be served very rare, so butterfly it thinly and sear for two minutes on each side.

Flat iron:

- Flat iron steak is found on the cow's shoulder blade.

- It is an inexpensive cut that can be a bit chewy, but the flavor is robust.

- This thick cut will take longer to cook but shouldn't be served beyond medium. Cook in a hot pan turned down to medium for eight minutes on each side.

Chateaubriand:

- Chateaubriand is the most expensive steak available and is found on the end of a fillet.

- It is tender and juicy with a texture like butter when properly prepared.

- Add a lot of butter to this extra lean cut of meat to break down the muscle fibers.

- Heat a hot pan and sear the steak on all sides and edges until each surface is golden brown.

- Finish in a 350-degree oven for 14 minutes and slice into 2-inch rounds before serving.

DRIVE A STICK SHIFT

Another man-card skill related to driving is knowing how to drive a stick shift, otherwise known as a vehicle with a manual transmission. Even though most cars these days have automatic transmissions, especially those available for rent, there will be a time when you'll need to drive a stick shift, whether it's your buddy's car or a moving van. Don't embarrass yourself by having to admit you don't know how to drive a manual vehicle.

- Familiarize yourself with the parts of a manual transmission. Know where to find the clutch (the pedal to the very left) and learn the stick shift pattern. Keep in mind that some makes such as Volkswagen may have their own patterns.

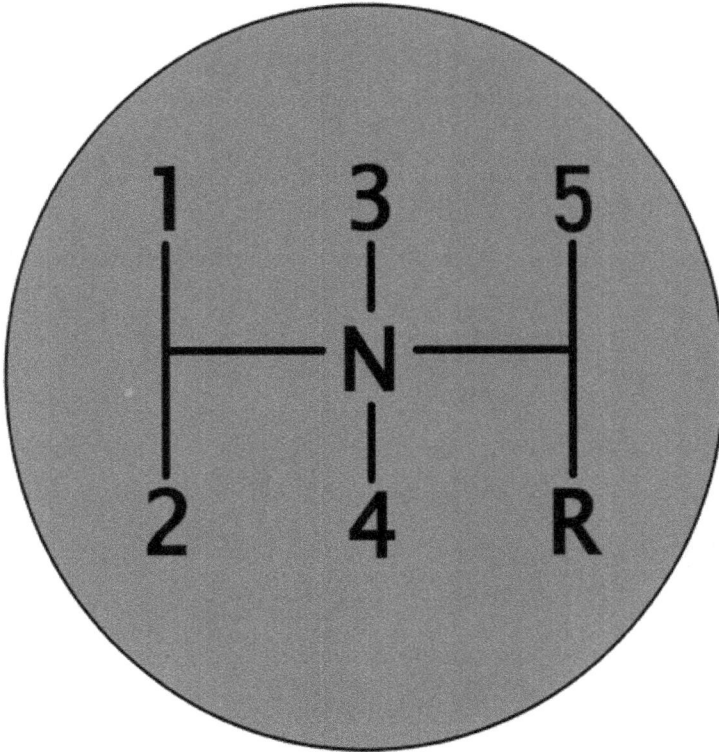

- With the gear shifter in the neutral position (N), press the clutch with your left foot all the way to the ground.

- Press the brake (middle pedal) with your right foot.

- Turn the ignition key.

- Disengage the emergency brake (also known as the parking or hand break).

- Move the gear shifter into first gear (1).

- Lift your right foot from the brake pedal.

- Slowly release the pressure on the clutch with your left foot. You may feel the vehicle start to move forward.

- As you release the clutch, use your right foot to gently and slowly press on the accelerator.

- Once you release the clutch entirely, you'll use your right foot to accelerate and brake as you drive in first gear.

- Continue to build speed until you reach the proper RPMs (revolutions per minute) to shift into second gear (between 2,500 and 3,000 RPMs).

- To shift into second gear, take your right foot off the accelerator at the same time as you depress the clutch with your left foot and shift the gear shifter into second gear (2).

- Repeat this process as you continue to build speed until you have run out of gears (usually five or six).

DRIVE WITH A TRAILER

Even if you've been driving a regular vehicle for years, driving with a trailer requires a whole new set of skills. It's not as simple as hitching up the trailer and heading down the road; missing even a single step in the process could severely compromise your safety. These tips from professional drivers are not only highly recommended but mandatory:

Familiarize yourself with the trailer you're towing. All trailers are different, and these nuances will affect the way you drive. For example, some trailers weigh more than the vehicle that's pulling them, which will greatly impact your stopping ability. Some travel trailers are taller as well, which means you'll have to pay more attention to height clearances.

Make wider turns around corners and curves. Your trailer's wheels will track closer to curbs than your truck's wheels, so you need to account for this as you turn; otherwise, you'll end up with your trailer wheels on the sidewalk.

Follow vehicles at a farther distance. You will require more stopping time because of the trailer's added weight. You will also need to begin braking earlier than usual to ensure you stop in time for red lights and stop signs.

Drive in the right lane whenever possible. If you need to brake suddenly, you'll be able to use the right shoulder to extend your stopping distance. This is also useful if you blow a tire so that you can pull over right away.

Adjust your trailer's brakes according to the load. If you're carrying something extremely heavy like a boat, you'll set your brakes to use a lot of force to stop. However, you won't need as much force when the trailer is empty, and if you keep the brakes adjusted for the heavier load, they will lock up, causing the trailer to skid.

Use lower gears to slow down on long downhills instead of riding the brakes. This will prevent your brakes from overheating and becoming ineffective.

Practice. As with most new skills, driving with a trailer takes practice. Take your trailer out when traffic is light so that you can get used to driving on roads without worrying about other vehicles.

CHANGE A TIRE

Changing a tire is one of those things that every driver should know, male or female, but women can probably get away with not knowing how to do it more than men. Men are often expected to come to the rescue when there's a flat tire, so instead of dialing AAA, follow these steps to change a tire on just about any vehicle:

Always have a fully inflated spare tire, car jack for your make and model, lug wrench, and your owner's manual in the car in case of a flat.

Slow down and pull over to a safe spot on the shoulder of the road or into a parking lot.

If you are on the side of the road, **turn your emergency flashers on** and apply the emergency brake.

If you have a reflective caution sign in an emergency kit, place it a few feet behind your vehicle.

Place a wheel wedge (large rock or stick) behind the tire opposite of the one that's flat. If your flat is on a rear tire, place the wedge behind the front tire and vice versa.

Remove your spare tire, jack, and lug wrench from your vehicle. Most of the time, these items will be in a compartment in your trunk.

Remove the hubcap (if there is one) from the damaged tire, and use the lug wrench to loosen the lug nuts (remember: lefty loosey!)

Consult your owner's manual to see where to place the jack. If you don't have the owner's manual, place it under a strong part of your vehicle's frame.

Turn the jack's handle clockwise until it lifts the flat tire a few inches off the ground.

Unscrew the lug nuts on the damaged tire. Store them in a safe place so that you don't lose them.

Remove the flat tire and lay it flat on the ground to prevent it from rolling away.

Place the spare tire onto the bolts that were exposed when you removed the flat.

Tighten the lug nuts by hand by turning them in a clockwise direction.

Lower the jack so that the tire rests on the ground but the full weight of the car isn't on the tire yet.

Use the lug wrench to tighten the lug nuts as much as you possibly can.

Lower the jack and remove it from under the car.

Place all tools and the flat tire back in the trunk.

Check the pressure of the spare tire, which should be 60 pounds per square inch.

JUMP-START
A CAR

Another vehicle-related skill that can get you or a friend out of a tricky situation is knowing how to jump-start a car. This is necessary when the energy in the car's battery runs too low to start the car. Fortunately, you can transfer the energy of another vehicle's battery to the dead one to get the car started. Here's how to do it correctly and safely:

Pull the vehicle with the good battery in front of or beside the one with the dead battery so that the engine compartments are close to each other.

Turn both vehicles off.

Open the hoods and locate the batteries for each vehicle.

Using jumper cables, connect one red clamp (+) to the positive (+) terminal on the dead battery.

Connect the other red clamp (+) to the positive (+) terminal on the working battery.

Connect one black clamp (-) to the negative (-) terminal on the working battery.

Attach the remaining black clamp (-) to an unpainted metal surface of the car with the dead battery.

Start the working car and let it run for a few minutes.

Start the car with the dead battery.

After a few minutes, remove the cables in the reverse order that you placed them (i.e., black clamp attached to metal, black clamp on negative terminal, red clamp on working battery, red clamp on dead battery).

Let the car with the dead battery run for at least 15 minutes before turning it off again.

FIX A LEAKY FAUCET

Plumbers are expensive, and the repairs they are called out for are often ones you can take care of yourself if you have the know-how. A leaky faucet is definitely a DIY repair that all men should be able to do. Not only will you have the satisfaction of completing the task yourself, but you'll also save a bunch of money!

Underneath the leaking sink, you'll find a small valve. Twist this counterclockwise to cut the water to the faucet.

Turn on the faucet and allow the water that's still in the system to drain into the sink.

Remove the faucet. You may need to look up your specific faucet model as this step differs for each design. In general, though, if there is a screw behind the handle, use an Allen wrench, or hex key, to remove the screw. If there's a top screw cover, use a flathead screwdriver to pry it off, then a Phillips head screwdriver to loosen the screw beneath the cover.

A shower or tub faucet may also require you to unscrew the faucet's faceplate from the wall and unscrew the metal sleeve over the shower valve.

Remove the faucet stem that regulates the hot and cold water. Use a wrench to loosen the packing nut located in the handle assembly, then pull the stem straight up and out.

The stem is usually the source of most faucet leaks. You can get the correct stem for your faucet at your local hardware store, but be sure you know your faucet's model number.

Clean the area around the handle and dry it with a clean cloth.

Replace any worn or damaged O-rings around the faucet housing.

Insert and align the new stem.

Reattach the faucet handle by reversing the steps you took to remove it.

Turn the water back on and check to ensure the leak has been fixed.

MOVE HEAVY STUFF

At least once in your life, you will be asked to help move someone's belongings, and of course, you'll probably have to move your own stuff several times. As a man, you're expected to provide the brawn during these moves and have the ability to pick up everything from light boxes to heavy furniture.

Don't worry about spending a ton of time in the weight room before helping someone move, though. There are techniques that can help you move heavy items without hurting your back.

Slide instead of lift. It's much easier to slide heavy furniture like sofas and armoires across the floor than to lift them. While there are commercial sliders available that you can slip under heavy objects to allow them to move easily across the floor, you can also use cardboard or plastic for moving items across carpet or felt for moving them across tile or wood floors.

If you don't have any sliders available, slip a moving blanket under two corners of the heavy object and another blanket under the other two corners.

Furniture straps or shoulder dollies can take the weight off your back and put it on your stronger muscle groups to make lifting and carrying heavy items easier. Professional movers use these all the time, so don't feel like you're weak if you use them too.

Dollies and hand trucks are great for moving heavy boxes that stack nicely on the dolly platform, but you can also use these to move upright objects like refrigerators and couches on end.

Use a mattress sling to move a mattress; although these objects might not be all that heavy, they are bulky and awkward. Make your own sling by threading a rope through the handles on the mattress and putting PVC pipe over the ends of the rope to create handles.

If you have to lift and carry heavy objects because you don't have any tools available:

- Use a "high-low" method to carry large objects. Tilt the object backwards and have one person carry the top and another person carry the bottom.
- Bend from the hips and knees, and use your core and legs to lift heavy items. Start in the squat position and lift from there to save your back.
- Turn chairs on their sides to create an *L* shape, which is easier to maneuver around corners and through narrow doorways.
- Remove legs and drawers if possible to make furniture lighter and more maneuverable.
- Empty furniture before trying to move it to make it lighter.

CALCULATE SQUARE FOOTAGE

Unless you're a scientist, mathematician, or engineer, you probably don't use a lot of the math you learned in school, but calculating square footage is definitely one thing you should remember how to do. You will need this skill numerous times in your life for things like determining how much paint, carpet, shingles, or other materials to buy or figuring out the dimensions of a room. Fortunately, calculating square footage is a simple formula: length x width.

- Measure one wall from end to end.
- Measure a wall that's perpendicular to the wall you just measured from end to end.

- Multiply the first measurement by the second measurement to get the square footage of the space.

- Example: Wall A is 12 feet and Wall B is 8 feet. 12 multiplied by 8 is 96, so the space is 96 square feet.

- Measure each space separately and calculate square footage separately. Then add all the numbers together to get total square footage.

- Example: If you have rooms that measure 96 square feet, 120 square feet, 48 square feet, and 135 square feet, the total square feet will be 96 + 120 + 54 + 135 = 405 square feet.

PAINT A STRAIGHT LINE

What separates a great painter from a good one is the ability to paint a straight line. If your lines are sloppy, people will know right away that an amateur painted them. This is particularly noticeable when you try to "cut in" the paint between a wall and a ceiling. These tips will ensure your lines look clean and professional:

- Use an angled brush. You won't get a straight line without one.

- Use only a small amount of paint on the brush.

- Do not try to "eyeball" it. Draw a reference line in pencil and paint along the line. The line, if visible, can be erased after the paint dries.

- Use an edger, especially in corners. Load the square pad with paint and run the edger along the surface, creating a straight painted line.

- If using an edger, make sure the wheels don't get paint on them. Otherwise, you'll have paint marks wherever the wheels rolled.

- If you're spraying paint on a surface, use a paint shield to prevent overspray.

- Use painter's tape to delineate a line. This is the best way to paint a straight line because you can place the tape wherever you want and make sure it's straight *before* you start painting. The tape will ensure you don't get paint anywhere except right where you want it.

- Make sure you let the paint fully dry before removing the tape.

- To prevent paint from seeping below the tape, apply a thin layer of clear or white caulking along the edge of the tape. You will want to carefully remove the tape before the paint completely dries if you use this technique.

- Touch up or redo areas that don't look good. Double-checking your work separates you from the amateurs who don't really care about the results.

MAINTAIN A RELATIONSHIP

There's nothing better in life than being in a healthy relationship with another person and going through the ups and downs together. Learning how to maintain a relationship so that it remains healthy is challenging, though. There's no perfect relationship, but you can use these tips to make sure yours stays as close to perfect as possible:

Put in the work. Relationships aren't always easy; they require constant work and attention. Only by working together toward a solid relationship can you get to the point where it seems easy.

Communicate. Arguments are going to happen, but it's *how* you argue that matters. Listen to the other person to really hear what they're saying instead of trying to formulate your response. Express what you're feeling so that your partner understands where you're coming from. Talking and listening form the foundation of a strong relationship.

Understand yourself. What do you need from a relationship to ensure you are emotionally able to positively contribute to your life together? Learn how to express your needs appropriately and how to regulate your emotions during arguments.

Set and respect boundaries. Let your partner know what you need from them to keep the relationship healthy. For example, you might need time with your friends or time alone. Similarly, you should find out what your partner needs to keep the relationship healthy and respect those needs.

Let go of control. Understanding that you can only control what *you* bring to the relationship and how you respond to your partner can go a long way in keeping a relationship healthy.

Reflect and learn. Each argument and subsequent resolution offers a learning opportunity that you can bring to your next conflict. Take time to think about what you did well to peacefully resolve the issue and what you could have done better so that you can apply your learnings to future situations. Additionally, think about the other relationships that work in your life and what makes them successful so that you can bring those positives to your new relationships.

DRESS FOR THE OCCASION

In an increasingly casual society, it might not seem critical that you know how to dress for every occasion, but how you dress says a lot about you, especially if you're on a date. You probably already know not to wear jeans to a black-tie event, but there are other guidelines that are more subtle.

Wear slacks and a dress shirt (long sleeved or short sleeved depending on the season) to religious ceremonies such as baptisms and bar mitzvahs.

A tuxedo is most appropriate for charity galas; formal weddings; and opera, ballet, or symphony openings. If the invitation says *formal*, get a tuxedo. If it says *black tie optional*, you can get away with a full suit.

Cocktail parties, most weddings, and engagement parties usually call for cocktail attire. For men, cocktail attire is a little vague, but you can never go wrong with a three-piece suit and dress shoes. Wear darker fabrics in the fall and winter and lighter choices in the spring and summer.

Holiday events typically include festive attire, which means you can have some fun with colors and fabrics. Suits are still the most appropriate option, but you can pair them with a brightly colored shirt or a themed tie. Sport coats or colorful cashmere sweaters are also appropriate choices for festive events.

Casual events such as outdoor weddings and garden parties allow you to trade out your slacks for chinos and your dress shirt for a polo or button-down shirt with short sleeves.

Backyard barbecues, family get-togethers, and birthday parties are usually casual, but stay away from sweatpants, basketball shorts, and graphic tees.

For dates, your destination will dictate your attire. Wear slacks and a dress shirt to a nice restaurant, black jeans and a polo shirt to a movie, and nice jeans and a solid-colored tee or polo for bowling or mini golf.

GIVE A BACK MASSAGE

Giving or receiving a back massage is a wonderful way to connect with your partner but only if you know how to give one properly. Your goal is to relax your partner's muscles and, therefore, their entire body. Don't rub too deeply unless your partner asks. For a simple, effective massage, follow these steps:

Prepare the massage space by covering your bed or couch with a towel that you don't mind getting oily.

Provide a couple of pillows to help make your partner more comfortable.

Warm up the oil by placing the bottle in a bowl of hot water.

Set the mood with soft music, low lighting, and candles.

Rub the oil in your hands and spread it across your partner's back in a figure-eight pattern to ensure their entire back is covered.

Start rubbing your partner's lower back, moving up toward the shoulders and back down.

Keep your back straight as you perform the massage, and use your body weight to create pressure instead of just your hands. Otherwise, your hands will tire quickly.

If your partner wants a deeper rub, use your knuckles and knead them into their skin.

Apply more pressure to the shoulders than you do to the back because the shoulders hold most of a person's tension.

Finish the massage by returning to the original figure-eight pattern. Lighten your pressure with each stroke.

Try massaging other parts of the body, such as legs, feet, arms, and hands for a full relaxation experience.

HOW TO LISTEN

As mentioned in the previous section on maintaining a relationship, listening is one of the top skills you need to make sure your relationships stay as healthy as possible. However, knowing how to listen is a vital skill for *all* aspects of your life. Train yourself to really hear the person talking instead of trying to think about what you're going to say when it's your turn. Here are some keys to becoming a better listener:

Face the speaker and maintain appropriate eye contact. Knowing how much eye contact is too much is dependent upon the situation, but a good rule is to maintain eye contact for about five seconds. When you look away, look to the side instead of up or down, which can signal that you want them to stop talking.

Pay attention to body language, which can be just as important as verbal language. You can gauge a person's emotions by what they are doing with their body. For example, if they're smiling, they are likely in a good mood and maybe even excited. If they have their arms crossed, they might feel upset and defensive.

Don't interrupt. This just causes frustration for the other person. It tells them that you think you are more important than they are. If you are naturally a quick thinker, force yourself to slow down and let the other person finish their thoughts.

Focus on what the other person is saying instead of just reacting. Your reaction can get in the way of hearing everything they have to say.

Don't prepare what you're going to say. You can't listen and prepare at the same time. If you need time to prepare, tell the other person that *after* they're done speaking.

Try to avoid giving advice and opinions unless the other person asks. Sometimes, all they want is a sympathetic ear, and they may be trying to come up with their own solutions.

Stay focused. Don't look at your phone or get distracted by other conversations going on around you.

Ask questions. Questions tell the other person that you're interested in what they said and want to know more. It also signals that you really hear what they're saying.

When the person has finished speaking, take time to paraphrase and summarize what they said. This allows them to correct anything you may have misunderstood or misheard. It also shows that you were paying attention, which is always something the other person wants to know.

READ BODY LANGUAGE

Not only is understanding body language an important part of being a good listener, but it's also a great way for you to learn what the other person is really thinking, even if they aren't saying it out loud. Start by learning how to read these five signs, then keep expanding your knowledge to become an expert:

Raised eyebrows. If a person raises their eyebrows for less than a second when you're speaking, it shows that they're interested in what you're saying. People raise their eyebrows quickly to agree with something, thank someone, or seek confirmation. It's basically a nonverbal way of saying "yes." In a romantic setting, raised eyebrows mean the person is happy to see you.

Head tilt. A head tilt exposes your neck to the other person, signifying that you're open. Since the neck is one of the most vulnerable parts of the body, when someone tilts their head, they are clearly comfortable enough with you to be vulnerable. When dating, a head tilt usually means they're interested in you; women use it much more than men do.

Mirroring is when you display the same body language as the person talking, and it's a great way to build rapport with the speaker. People only mirror the body language of people they like, and you probably already do this with friends without realizing it. Professionally, you can use this body language in sales and marketing to help you connect with customers.

Fidgeting. If someone is fidgeting with other objects such as a necklace, keys, toys, etc., while you're talking, they're probably bored. Change up your delivery or speech to re-engage them. If you want to end a conversation, this is a surefire way to do it.

Crossed arms create a barrier between that person and the speaker. It's a defensive position that indicates the person feels threatened, angry, or anxious. If someone crosses their arms while talking to you, try giving them something to hold to open up their arms and (subconsciously) their mind.

ADMIT YOU'RE WRONG

No one likes to be wrong, but we're human. Being wrong is part of how we learn in life, and it happens all the time. Even so, it's difficult to admit when you're wrong as society has ingrained in us the idea that being wrong is emasculating. Nothing could be further from the truth, though, especially as you strive to become a better person with every interaction. These steps will help you admit that you're wrong and keep relationships intact:

Agree with what the other person is saying. For example, say, "You're right. I haven't been pulling my weight with the household chores, even on days when I don't work."

Pause. This is an important step to allow the other person to hear you admit that you were wrong. They may jump in with more accusations, which you agree about again and pause again. This also helps them know you aren't being defensive and are truly admitting you were wrong.

Give your rationale or lesson learned. Note that your rationale should *not* be an excuse but instead a glimpse into your thought process. For instance, say, "I thought I deserved a break from chores because I've been working so hard, but after talking to you, I realize that you've been working hard too. If we do them together, we both get more free time."

Allow the other person to have the final word. Use your newfound listening skills to really hear what the other person is saying. Usually, the other person won't have much to say because you've said it all for them. But they might say "thank you" or provide you with guidance on how to proceed from here. Either way, your actions will end the conflict.

HOW TO APOLOGIZE

Now that you've admitted you're wrong, you might have to apologize as well. This is another skill that society has made more difficult than it needs to be by making people who apologize seem weak. Again, this is just not the case. In fact, it takes a lot of strength to apologize, and if you do it in the right way, you'll earn a lot of respect in the other person's eyes.

Say "I'm sorry." This is the first step; just verbalizing the words is disarming and can diffuse a tense situation. Don't use a substitute phrase like "I feel awful." Be direct and open about the fact that you're sorry. Words matter.

Specifically state what you're apologizing for. This shows that you understand what you did that caused the other person harm and that you're not just *saying* you're sorry to end the conversation.

Demonstrate that you understand how your behavior affected the other person. This requires a little extra effort than just saying you're sorry without an explanation, which is why it's such an important part of a good apology.

Demonstrate how you're going to prevent the mistake from happening again. An apology doesn't mean much without changed behavior.

Make reparations if necessary. For instance, if your actions caused someone a loss of money, repay that person promptly and in full.

Here's an example of a good apology: "I'm sorry my dog got muddy footprints all over your sofa. I understand that you want your things to be nice when other people come over, and I didn't take precautions to ensure he didn't jump up on the sofa. In the future, I will make sure my dog stays outside or I won't bring him at all when I visit your house. I'll pay to have your sofa cleaned since I caused the issue."

ACCEPT CRITICISM

Getting criticized for something is akin to admitting you were wrong, and it's not easy to accept, especially if you're criticized over something you've put a lot of effort into. However, as growing, progressing humans, criticism is just as important as praise. It gives you an opportunity to improve and move closer to your goals. Here's how to accept criticism and show others you care about improving yourself:

> **Pause.** This is essential because the automatic impulse is to react to criticism, usually emotionally. This pause will give you time to process what you're being told, and it gives you a chance to remain calm. At this point, you should also be aware of your facial expressions and adjust them accordingly.

> **Keep an open mind.** Try to think about the situation from their point of view. What might look perfect to you could be causing problems elsewhere without you even knowing it. It's also important to remember that constructive criticism can come from anywhere, at any level, so receiving criticism from someone you don't expect might be even

more valuable than criticism coming from people who are above you.

Listen. Again with the listening thing! Knowing how to listen is applicable everywhere, and it's vital when taking criticism. Let the person giving the criticism have their say without interrupting them. Then repeat what they said to give them a chance to correct anything you misunderstood.

Thank them. Yes, *thank them*. Showing appreciation for their evaluation and criticism will keep your relationship with the person intact, even if you don't agree with the feedback. If they didn't care about you, they wouldn't bother giving you suggestions on how to approve.

Ask questions. Take the time to really understand the issue by asking clarifying questions and seeking suggestions for how to resolve the issue. You might even ask for examples so that you have a better idea of how to alter your behavior in the future.

Follow up. If you don't agree with the criticism, you can simply say, "Thanks for bringing this to my attention," and close the conversation. If the criticism is valid and necessary for improvement, though, ask to follow up with their concerns at a later date.

ACCEPT COMPLIMENTS

Even though we don't take criticism well from others, we are usually really good at taking it from *ourselves*. That's why accepting compliments can sometimes be challenging. When someone else says something nice about you, it's easy to brush the compliment off, crack a joke, or even tell them all the things you did wrong instead.

When someone gives you a compliment, realize it's not about how you feel about yourself. It's about how others perceive you. It's supposed to make you feel good about something you've done or a part of who you are, so don't overthink it. It's not going to come off as bragging or being full of yourself to accept a compliment.

Just say thank you. That's it. You don't have to expand on your thoughts, agree with the compliment, or return one of your own compliments. Simply tell the other person you appreciate the kind words and move on. You can worry about confronting your own negative thoughts about yourself later as that's a much bigger undertaking.

STAND UP FOR OTHERS

These days, the bullying and shaming of others is more rampant than ever, especially on social media platforms. The effects of bullying and shaming are far reaching, and it will only stop if others take action. This is why standing up for others is one of the most important things you can do to better the world. However, it's not always easy to do, particularly when it's easier not to get involved at all. As the old saying goes, though, "The only thing necessary for evil to triumph in the world is that good men do nothing." Therefore, it's important to learn how to stand up for others and, in the process, stand up for your own beliefs as well.

Consider the values you believe are important enough to stand up for. This will help you know when it's time to insert yourself into a situation.

Trust your judgment. You might not have time to fully assess a situation before coming to the assistance of another person, but your brain knows what's right and what's wrong according to your belief system. Your instincts are almost never wrong.

Decide on the action you're going to take. What are you going to do to show your support? Are you going to agree with an unpopular decision? Are you going to write a letter on someone else's behalf? Are you going to quit a job because another person got fired unjustly? How far are you willing to go? Just remember that once you're in, you need to be in all the way.

Defend appropriately. Don't just defend your friends because they're your friends. If they're truly wrong and you know it, your support will backfire on both of you.

Don't be aggressive, but don't be quiet either. Say something like, "This needs to stop right now."

Encourage others to stand up as well. The more voices that band together, the quicker the bullying or shaming will stop.

Report inappropriate behaviors. If you don't want to get directly involved with a situation, take action another way by reporting inappropriate actions. Many times, anonymous reporting can stop the behavior and result in consequences for the bully.

PRESENT TO A GROUP

No matter how hard you try to put off presenting in front of a group, there will come a time that you'll have to demonstrate something to others, whether it's to a few people where you work or a crowd of at a conference. While it's natural to be nervous, even if it's your 100th presentation, there are some tips to keep in mind to ensure your presentation is well received and memorable.

Prepare and practice. The more time you take ahead of the presentation to write out exactly what you're going to say and practice saying it, the better your presentation will be. Don't try to come up with your presentation the night before it's scheduled and expect to pull off a flawless performance.

Keep it simple. Identify the key takeaways you want your audience to have, and focus on making those ideas as clear as possible. This will also help you reach as diverse an audience as possible. Remember that audiences want to be able to understand and apply what you're presenting, so enable them to do that by cutting out any unnecessary and complicated information.

Put yourself in your audience's shoes. Think about what your audience would want when creating your presentation. This will help keep the order of ideas logical and cohesive. It will also ensure that you don't leave anything critical out.

Use visual aids. Add pictures, graphics, and videos to your presentation where appropriate to keep your audience engaged. Long slides full of text are difficult and boring to read.

Don't read straight off slides. Your audience can read; your job is to expand on what's presented on the slides. Place only your main points on the slide, and provide details orally.

Use note cards or the speaker note section on slides to keep your place.

Make sure all your equipment works ahead of time. When technology lets you down, it's hard to refocus on your presentation.

Smile and make eye contact with your audience.

Be aware of your body language.

Show your passion, which will be contagious to your audience.

Tell anecdotes to loosen up the audience and illustrate how your topic applies to real life.

Breathe deeply if you start to get nervous, and remember that the audience is focused on your material, not on you.

TELL A JOKE

While everyone loves a good joke, not everyone knows how to tell one in a way that will get the most laughs. After all, if it were easy, everyone would be a comedian. Telling a joke is an art form; you might not perfect it, but you can at least learn how to tell a joke to lighten the mood, no matter where you are.

Know your audience. Not every joke is appropriate for every situation. Even if joking is your way of dealing with your nervousness, it's important that you know when a joke will be appreciated and when it's better to remain serious.

Take your cues from other jokes. If you're not sure whether your joke is appropriate, wait for others to joke around to see if the mood is right for your joke. If not, save it for another time.

Practice the setup. Think of a joke as a short story. Your audience needs to know the who, what, where, and when of your joke so that they can follow it to the punchline.

Invest in your joke. Put some of yourself into it, including your own twists and personality so that it's truly *your* joke and not just something you've memorized.

Keep a straight face. Unless the joke relies on pratfall or facial expressions, try to keep a straight face as you tell it. Deadpan delivery always seems to make a joke funnier than one that's told in a joking manner. Present your material as fact for the biggest laughs.

Wait for your audience. Never laugh at your own joke, and remember that it might take a few seconds for your audience to "get" the punchline, especially if your reference is a bit obscure.

Let your audience laugh. Give them time to respond to one joke before telling another.

COMMUNICATE
WITH A BARBER

Your hair is a major part of your identity, so knowing how to communicate with your barber is necessary to get the haircut you want. Otherwise, you might have to deal with a bad haircut for several weeks before you can fix it. Here's how to make sure your barber understands exactly what you want them to do:

Find a photo. This is the best way to show your barber how you want your hair to turn out, especially if you're changing your hairstyle to something new.

Understand that you won't look exactly like a photo. It's okay to want a specific hairstyle, but your bone structure, hair type, and other factors might make it difficult to achieve. Ask your barber questions about the style you've chosen to make sure they're going to be able to give you what you expect.

Be specific. If you don't have a picture to show your barber, make sure you're very specific about what you want. Show them with your hands where you want extra trimming. Don't just say, "A little more off the side, please."

Learn haircut lingo. Words like *fade, taper, thin, layer,* and *buzz* can help you better describe what it is you want your hair to look like when the barber is done.

Know the length you want your hair to be after the cut is done. Remember that your barber can always make your hair shorter, but they can't make it longer. Be prepared to tell your barber to stop when your hair gets to the length you want it to be, and keep in mind that wet hair appears longer, so it will shorten up as it dries.

Show your barber how you style your hair on a regular day and tell them what products you use. This will help them visualize your cut and provide advice on new styles and options.

Defer to the expert. Your barber has the experience and knowledge to help you get the type of hairstyle that looks best on your face shape and bone structure.

BUY SOMEONE ELSE CLOTHES

The advice is simple on this one: just don't. Don't buy someone else clothes unless you know exactly what they want. This is because people's tastes in clothing are as varied as their personalities. Of course, there might be times when buying someone else clothes is necessary, so if you find yourself in a must-do situation, follow these tips:

Know their style. The better you know someone, the easier it will be to buy them clothing they will not only keep but also love. If you don't know their style, look at their social media posts to figure out their interests and preferences.

Know their size. This is even trickier than knowing their style. If you get something that's the wrong size, they won't be able to wear it. If you don't know the other person's size, ask them or someone who definitely knows. Another idea is to find someone with a similar build and ask them what size they are; this can be a sensitive topic, though, so be careful.

Pay attention. When you're out and about with a person, pay attention to the clothing items they look at and what they buy for themselves. This is the best way to ensure you get something they like in the size they wear.

ASK FOR A RAISE

Money is always a tricky thing to talk about with anyone but especially so with your boss. Asking for a raise can be intimidating, but if you truly deserve more money, sometimes you have to bring the subject up yourself.

Make a list of your accomplishments over the last six months or since you last had a raise. Be sure to describe how you have positively impacted your organization, and use statistics if possible. The stronger the data you present, the harder it is for your boss to say no.

Use salary reports to establish a competitive salary for your position. Keep in mind that averages are just that: averages. The size of your company, your total benefit package, and the industry you're in will all impact the final number.

Explain how giving you a raise will positively affect your boss. They don't really care about why you need the extra money; they care about what they will get in return. Talk about your personal goals and how they align with the company's objectives. Draw a straight line from your raise to overall company performance.

Show confidence. Even if you aren't confident, your outward appearance needs to show that you are. As long as you have supporting evidence and you're prepared to answer their questions, you'll reflect a confident attitude that supports the idea that you deserve a raise.

Put your request in writing. In most cases, your boss won't be the only one who needs to sign off on your raise. Make it easy for them to demonstrate your value to others by putting your raise request in writing along with all the supporting evidence.

Ask if you can follow up. If you don't get an answer right away (and chances are that you won't), ask if it's okay for you to follow up in two weeks if you haven't heard anything. That way, your boss knows that you aren't going to just let it go and that they need to take action.

Be prepared for a rejection. There may be factors outside of your control that are behind a negative answer. If that happens, ask what you can do to be considered for a raise in the future. Effective bosses will provide feedback and help you make a career plan to reach your goals.

Remain professional. Whether the answer is yes or no, remaining professional will help you down the road when you ask for future raises. Bragging about your raise to others will make your boss regret giving you the raise and create conflict among the other employees.

SPEAK A FOREIGN LANGUAGE

Learning a foreign language as an adult isn't easy. We all have busy lives, and sometimes our brains don't seem to have room for new skills like this. However, learning to speak a new language is good for us because it keeps our brains flexible and open to new skills. The best way to learn a foreign language is to immerse yourself in a community that only uses that language, but that's not always possible. Here are some other ways to become bilingual:

Use an app or take a course. There are several language-learning apps available that can teach you the basics of a new language. You can also find reasonably priced language courses at community colleges or community centers.

Set goals. As with anything, having goals for learning a new language will motivate you to do the work necessary to achieve them. Be sure to write down your goals and put them somewhere you can see them to keep your eye on the prize.

Learn the 1,000 top words in the target language first. To be conversational, you need between 1,000 and 3,000 words in your basic vocabulary. Don't waste your time trying to learn words you'll rarely use until you've mastered the basics.

Repetition is key. Repeated exposure to words and phrases is the best way to cement them in your brain. Use physical or digital flashcards to ensure you are exposed to your growing vocabulary on a regular basis.

Use mnemonic devices, gestures, and visualization to help you remember the meanings of words. Whenever you associate a word with something else like a gesture or an image, you're more likely to recall that word when you need it.

Think in the foreign language whenever possible. Translating in your brain slows down the speaking process, so practice thinking in the target language to reduce errors and speed up conversation.

Use your language all day, every day. Certainly, this might not be possible at all times, but the more you use it, the more comfortable you'll be with it. Tape new words on items in your house, change your phone's language to the target language, take your flashcards with you and study them whenever you can, and listen to audiobooks in the target language as you commute.

Get a language partner. Find someone who is learning the same language and get together frequently to practice using the language in practical situations.

TRAVEL TO A FOREIGN PLACE

Traveling abroad is not the same as traveling domestically, especially in post-pandemic times. While traveling itself doesn't require any special skill, traveling to a foreign country does, especially if you don't want to look like the typical tourist.

Know what documents are required. You'll definitely need a passport, but you might also need a visa, proof of vaccinations, or other documents depending on where you're traveling. Research the requirements and give yourself enough time to make sure you obtain all the necessary documents before your travel date.

Research the country you're traveling to. This is the best way to avoid looking like a tourist. Understand the customs, traditions, and culture of the country, and if possible, learn at least enough of the language to ask for directions and order a meal.

Know what you're getting yourself into. If you don't like living in rudimentary conditions, don't choose a country that doesn't offer all the comforts of home. If you don't like hiking, don't choose a country where hiking is the primary attraction. Again, as with everything related to traveling to a foreign country, research, research, research.

Know how to get emergency assistance if you need it. This might involve the consulate or embassy for your country. It also involves knowing where the closest hospital is to your accommodations and how to call the police or emergency services in the country you travel to.

Don't overpack. Take only what you need; traveling light is a major advantage when going abroad. There's no need to bring three changes of clothing for every day that you're there, especially because you can do laundry if necessary.

Don't expect to have cellular service everywhere you go. We've become pretty dependent on cellular phones, but some countries aren't there yet. Make sure you're prepared to be out of communication for a while, and let the people back home know this too. Bring a portable battery as well; electrical outlets aren't everywhere.

Consider travel insurance. Before the pandemic, this would have been a take-it-or-leave-it suggestion, but you never know when something out of your control will arise that interrupts your trip. The small amount of money required for insurance is well worth the peace of mind it gives.

Deal with jet lag. Don't take a nap when you get where you're going. This only prolongs the misery and prevents you from getting on schedule. Get plenty of rest before you leave, drink lots of water on the plane, and choose an easy activity for when you arrive.

ASK FOR HELP

Another skill that society has deemed a weakness is asking for help, and again, we're here to tell you that not only is it *not* a weakness, it's actually a sign of emotional intelligence. Nothing is more manly than knowing when you need help and asking for it.

Pick the right time to ask. You're more likely to get a receptive response when you wait for a good time to ask for help. This means waiting until the other person isn't busy or about to leave. If you are unsure when to ask, say, "I'd love to ask for your help with something. When would be a good time to chat?"

Speak up. If you don't ask for help, you probably won't receive it. People aren't mind readers, and they can't always tell if you're struggling. Even if they do think you're having trouble, they might hesitate to step in because they don't want to intrude.

Be specific. Again, people can't read your mind. Just saying, "I need help," doesn't provide much direction. Instead, be specific about what you need help with.

Keep it positive. Frame your question in a positive way that compliments the person you're asking for help. For example, say, "I'm really struggling with this report, and you handled it so quickly. Do you have a moment to give me some tips?"

Don't put yourself down. Rather than insulting yourself for not understanding something or not being able to get everything done, just say, "This is challenging for me, but I know I'll be able to do it with your help."

Be persistent. You might have to reach out to more than one person to get the help you need. This is okay, and it's often the best way to get several perspectives.

Help others when they ask. People are more willing to help you if you have helped them in the past.

Thank others for the help, even if you didn't quite get what you needed. You don't want to discourage them from helping you or another person in the future.

BUY A GOOD SUIT

Every man should have at least one suit that makes them feel confident and self-assured, no matter the occasion. One good suit can be worn for weddings, funerals, interviews, and most other informal events. However, you do have to put down some money for a suit that both gives you confidence and lasts a long time.

Visit a store that specializes in men's suits. The salespeople at these stores are trained and experienced in helping men select the right suit with the proper fit.

You might not know exactly what you're looking for in a suit when you go shopping, and that's okay, but you should have an idea of your tastes and preferences. Knowing what event you're getting the suit for is important, but if you're just looking for a suit to wear anywhere, you should at least know your color preference as a starting point.

The suit material doesn't matter much, especially for a first suit. Going with a traditional wool suit is probably your best bet here. There are many premium materials that you might consider for subsequent suits, but wool will look good and last forever. Of course, you might want a thinner material for a spring or summer suit and a thicker one for fall or winter, but wool comes in various thicknesses, so stick with wool until you're ready to splurge a little more.

Navy and charcoal suits are most popular right now, and having one of each allows you to mix and match the pants and coats.

Off-the-rack suits are fine, but you should have at least one suit that's tailored to fit you perfectly. Don't worry about gaining or losing weight as tailored suits can be easily taken in or let out. The fit is the most important factor in choosing a suit, which is why going to a specialty store is the key to getting the right suit and fit.

BUILD A GOOD CREDIT SCORE

People don't often think about their credit scores until they need to purchase something major with a loan or mortgage. By then, if you haven't paid attention to it, your score can be really low, making it difficult to buy the things you want or need. You should start monitoring your credit score as soon as you have your first bank account, but if it's too late for that, start doing it now. If your credit is low or you don't have any credit yet, these tips will help you get it in shape:

Pay every loan you have on time, every time. Late and skipped payments cause the biggest hit to your credit score. With automatic payment options, there's really no reason to miss or be late on payments, so set them up for every bill you can pay online and watch your credit score rise.

Don't "max out" your credit cards. Your credit score is partially based on how much debt you have in relation to your credit. Experts recommend that you keep your debt at around 30 percent of your total credit limit.

Pay your balances off every month. This will give you a higher credit score than paying the minimum on time every month.

A long credit history will increase your scores. This is because lenders look for patterns and behaviors over time. The more information you have to demonstrate your credit worthiness, the higher your credit rating will be.

Only apply for credit that you actually need. Opening a lot of credit accounts at once signals to the credit reporting agencies that your economic situation may have changed and that you're going to have to rely on credit for a time.

Monitor your credit report to make sure no one has stolen your identity and used it to make purchases that they never paid for. You can get a free credit report from each of the three major credit reporting agencies once a year, and the internet has made it easy for you to request them.

Realize that every time your credit is checked by a lender, your credit rating goes down. This is because the credit reporting agencies believe you are going to owe money soon, which increases the likelihood of you defaulting, even if you can and will make every payment on time.

READ BOOKS

Once you get out of school and are no longer forced to read books, it can be challenging to read anything other than what you need for work or other pursuits. However, reading is something we should all be doing more of as adults to expand our thinking, improve memory and connections in the brain, reduce stress, and prevent age-related cognitive decline. In other words, we become smarter when we read, and reading also keeps our brains healthy.

Even if you love to read, finding the time to do it is the hard part. Keep in mind, though, that some of the most successful people in the world, including Warren Buffet, Mark Cuban, and Elon Musk, read at least one book a week. They make the time for it, and their example can help you find the same type of success. Here's what they do to read more books:

Prioritize reading. Make it your preferred way to learn new things; if you don't, other activities will always take precedence over reading.

Set a reading goal. As with everything you want to improve, it's necessary to set specific goals. If you just say, "I want to read more," you probably won't make much progress, but if you say, "I am going to read at least one book a week," then you have a concrete goal that you can measure.

Reading one book a week takes about 30 minutes a day, depending on the length of the book. It shouldn't be too difficult to carve out 30 minutes to read each day. A great time for this is right before you go to bed. Instead of watching screens and trying to sleep, grab a book and wind down for a half hour by reading.

Reconsider how you currently spend your time to find more time for reading. Some things that you do now might not be as productive or constructive as reading. For instance, could you spend less time checking your emails every day? Maybe you could check your emails once in the morning and once in the afternoon and use the time you saved to read instead.

Always have a book with you wherever you go. You never know when you'll have some time to read. We spend a lot of time waiting during our daily lives; instead of checking your phone or playing a game on it, take the opportunity to read.

Read only what you love. If you aren't enjoying a book, stop reading it and grab something else. You'll stop reading altogether if you're reading books you don't like. Forcing yourself to read something you don't enjoy will only make it seem like a chore instead of a pastime.

Always have a list of books you want to read. When you're finished with one book, it should be easy to select the next one right away. Otherwise, you might put off looking for one and stop reading.

Buy several books in advance. This will help you keep reading because you've already spent the money on the books. If you don't read them, it's a waste of money, and no one likes wasting money.

Choose audiobooks if you have a hard time reading actual books. It's not cheating, and you're getting the same information that you would if you read the paper version. If you are an auditory learner, audiobooks might be the best option for you.

Limit distractions by creating a place where you can focus as you read, and put a book everywhere you might have a moment of free time. Even if you're reading several books at once, you'll still get more out of reading than if you don't read at all.

WHISTLE WITH
YOUR FINGERS

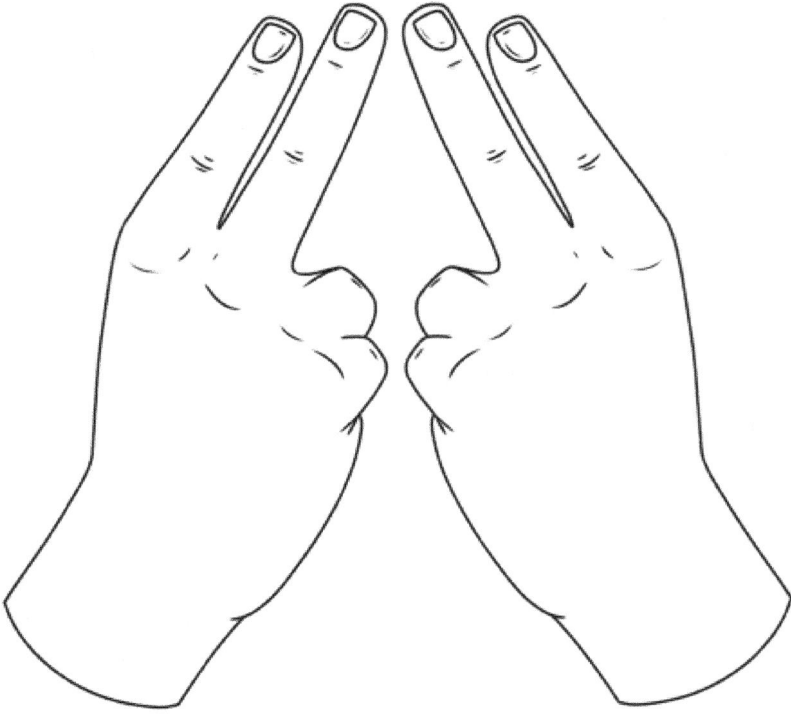

Whether you need to call your kids home from down the street or hail a cab in New York City, knowing how to whistle with your fingers makes the task much easier. Plus, since this seems to be a dying skill, your friends will turn in amazement when you let out an ear-piercing whistle that gets the attention of everyone within a block's distance or further!

Choose the fingers you're going to use. The most popular fingers are the forefinger and middle finger of each hand. Position them in an *A* shape with the tips of your middle fingers touching.

Wet your lips and tuck them over your teeth (as if you're pretending to be an old man without any teeth). Your fingers will press down on your lower lip to keep it folded over your teeth, but you'll need to keep your upper lip folded over without this help.

Take your fingers in the *A* shape and push back your tongue with the tips. To do this properly, put your fingertips under your tongue and push the tip of your tongue back so that you are essentially folding a quarter of your tongue over on itself. Then push your tongue back until your first knuckles reach your bottom lip.

Keeping the tip of your tongue folded back and lips tucked over your teeth, close your mouth over your fingers and blow.

You should feel the air go out over your bottom lip and nowhere else. If you feel the air escaping from the sides of your mouth, create a tighter seal around your fingers with your mouth. Your tongue should not come out between your fingers because that means it's blocking the air.

Practice. You might not be able to make a loud whistle right away; it can take some time to get the perfect finger and tongue placement. Make sure you practice in an area where you're alone so that you don't annoy anyone else.

DANCE

While you can avoid knowing how to dance when you're in middle or high school, you can't get away with it forever. You will need to know how to dance at your wedding and other events throughout your life. You don't want to make a fool out of yourself on the dance floor, but you also don't want to be a wallflower. Learn one of these basic partner dances to impress your date and other people who might not expect you to have such smooth moves.

Waltz:

- This is the easiest partner dance to learn because it's slow and only uses four steps. It's in three-quarter time, so you can easily recognize songs to waltz to as well.

- To lead a waltz, follow these steps:
  - With your feet hip-distance apart, step forward with your left foot and move your body in that direction.
  - Move your right foot sideways to the right.
  - Bring your left foot close to your right so that they're parallel to each other and almost touching.
  - Step back with your right foot.
  - Take one step back and to the left with your left foot.
  - Bring your right foot next to your left so that they're parallel to each other and almost touching.
  - Repeat.

East Coast Swing:

- The East Coast Swing is the easiest of all swing dances and will set you up to learn more complicated dances.
- To lead the East Coast Swing, follow these steps:
    - Start with your left foot.
    - Triple step to the left (i.e., left, right, left).
    - Triple step to the right (i.e., right, left, right).
    - Step backward with your left foot.
    - Shift weight to your right foot.
    - Repeat.

PLAY AN INSTRUMENT

If your parents made you learn an instrument when you were growing up, count yourself lucky. Music and happiness have a direct correlation to each other, and when you know how to create music instead of just listening to it, your enjoyment of life increases significantly. Plus, learning how to read music is another one of those skills that keeps your brain young and staves off age-related dementia.

There are literally hundreds of musical instruments you can learn to play, but if you're looking to start making music sooner rather than later, give these instruments a try:

Harmonicas are probably the easiest instrument to learn to play quickly because you don't have to worry about a note not being in key. This is because each harmonica is keyed to a different scale, so if you want to change keys, you have to change harmonicas. Harmonicas are also small enough to fit in your pocket, so you can take one everywhere you go and practice whenever you have time.

Guitar. Learning to play the guitar is a dream for many young people who have musical aspirations. This is because some of the coolest people in history have played the guitar, and we always want to emulate cool people. There's also the fact that the guitar is fairly easy to learn because it's all about memorizing finger positions. There are plenty of online lessons for guitars as well, including the most basic instructions for true beginners. Of course, proficiency can take a lot longer, but if you can play your favorite songs, you'll at least be a rock star in your own mind.

Percussion instruments. Let's face it: Banging on a drum doesn't seem that hard. Certainly, becoming a master percussionist is much more difficult than hitting a drum in time to the beat, but it's a good place to start if you've never played an instrument before. You don't even have to know how to read music to play the cowbell, castanets, bongos, tambourine, and other percussion instruments.

If you really want to make an impression, learn to play an obscure instrument like the toha, balalaika, theremin, cimbalom, glass armonica, crwth, hang, nyckelharpa, yaybahar, pyrophone, or didgeridoo. You'll seem eminently cool, and you'll have a fun conversation starter as well!

TAKE GOOD PICTURES

These days, everyone has a camera in their hand, but that doesn't mean that the quality of photos is getting any better. If anything, it's getting worse because people are snapping shots of everything and not taking light and composition into consideration, both of which are essential for good photos. The best pictures come from high-quality single-lens reflex cameras, but even if you only have a phone, you can still get wall-worthy prints by following these tips:

Turn on the gridlines feature and remember the "rule of thirds." This is a principle that says any image should be broken down into thirds, both vertically and horizontally, so that there are nine parts of an image in total. The gridlines on a phone's camera app allow you to place the most interesting parts of an image in the intersections to create a more balanced and level photo.

Manually focus your camera. Auto focus is great for images that have the most important object in the foreground, but if your image doesn't have an obvious subject, adjusting the focus manually will ensure you get the picture you want. To manually focus your phone's camera, tap the screen where you want your lens to focus to make that section sharper.

Use natural light as much as possible. Very few smartphone photos that are taken with a flash can be considered high quality. They are often overexposed or blurry, and the subjects look washed out. Even after dark, you can find natural light that will allow you to experiment with shadows, creating bold, dramatic photographs. You can also use your phone's editing app to experiment with the exposure settings to alter photographs until they're perfect.

Focus on a single subject. Spend some time setting up your shot by experimenting with subject placement. Some professional photographers believe that two thirds of the photo should be negative space and that your subject shouldn't fill up more than one third of the frame. This helps your subject really stand out.

Hold your phone still. This might be the hardest part of taking a good photograph with your phone because phones are designed to be *mobile*. Steady yourself against a wall or another person if you must hold your phone. If at all possible, set your phone up against a solid object and use the timer to keep your phone completely still. A tripod is an even better option.

Experiment with different perspectives. Taking the same picture from various angles and playing with negative space can really enhance your subject.

Avoid zooming in. It's always better to get closer to your subject than to zoom in on it, which can make the resulting photograph grainy or pixelated.

Take candid pictures. The one good thing about film cameras is the inability to delete pictures when you think they won't turn out the way you want. Candid shots are disappearing, which is a shame since they've historically been some of the most treasured photographs people have.

Don't be afraid to edit. Filtering, removing blemishes, and playing with light and exposure can make your photographs even more compelling. Just because you've changed the photo somewhat doesn't make it any less "real."

RECITE A POEM FROM MEMORY

For many women, nothing is more romantic than a man reciting poetry from memory. There's something enchanting about a man who has taken the time to memorize their favorite poem and knows how to deliver it in a meaningful way. It also adds a bit of "wow" factor to a conversation when you unexpectedly sprinkle in a few lines of poetry. Here's a list of the best poems to memorize. Pick your favorite and learn it until it's cemented in your brain.

- "Nothing Gold Can Stay" by Robert Frost
- "Death Be Not Proud" by John Donne
- "Casey at the Bat" by Ernest Lawrence Thayer
- "The Road Not Taken" by Robert Frost
- "Ode to a Nightingale" by John Keats
- "Because I could not stop for Death" by Emily Dickinson
- "Annabel Lee" by Edgar Allen Poe
- "Oh Captain! My Captain!" by Walt Whitman
- "Ode to a Grecian Urn" by John Keats
- "Do not go gentle into that good night" by Dylan Thomas
- "Charge of the Light Brigade" by Alfred Lord Tennyson
- "The New Colossus" by Emma Lazarus

- Any sonnet by Shakespeare but especially Sonnet #18 ("Shall I compare thee to a summer's day?")

HAVE GOOD HANDWRITING

In today's digital world, it might seem like good handwriting is an obsolete skill. We definitely don't write things by hand as often as we used to, but it's still important to have good handwriting skills for several reasons. One reason is that writing things down improves your memory; you're less likely to forget something when you write it down. Second, handwriting keeps your fine motor skills strong. Third, typing on a keyboard and handwriting require very different cognitive processes; handwriting requires more brain power than pressing keys and making the letters appear on the screen.

More importantly, your handwriting is unique to *you*. It's part of your legacy and a way to literally leave your mark on the world. Your grandchildren and great-grandchildren will marvel at seeing your handwriting on notes, letters, reminders, and the backs of photographs. Don't neglect this skill. If you need to improve your handwriting, know that it's still possible even as an adult.

Choose the right pen. Most of us use pens with a barrel that's too small to really control well. Try a fatter pen for better control over forming the letters. You should also consider how fast the ink flows from the pen. If it's too fast for your writing pace, you'll have smeared ink everywhere.

Sit up straight. Posture matters when it comes to handwriting. Keep your feet flat on the floor, your back straight, and your hand and arm relaxed. Your forearm should rest comfortably on the table.

While you're working on improving your handwriting, work on wide-ruled paper so that you have space to form the letters properly. You can shrink your letters back down once you've made the improvements you want.

Slow down. Now that we're used to typing, we often try to write as fast as we type. This just leads to messy writing and ill-formed letters.

Pay attention to the height of your letters. They each need to be the correct height in relation to the other letters. If some of your letters are the wrong height, your writing will be cramped and hard to read.

Find a style you like and copy it. If there is a handwriting style you want to emulate, get some tracing paper and trace it until you can imitate it on your own.

Journal. You need to practice your handwriting or it will deteriorate just like any other skill. A journal gives you ample space to practice, and you can try out different styles all in one place.

Stick to it. Change never happens overnight. If you truly want to improve your handwriting, you must keep working at it until you get it right. Even after you get it right, you will need to continue to write to maintain your skills.

WRITE A LETTER

As with handwriting, writing a letter is somewhat of a lost art, especially when all you need to reach someone is a text or email.

Again, though, knowing how to write a letter properly is something you should know how to do when the need arises. Keep in mind that people still love to receive letters in the mail, even if it doesn't happen as often as it used to. You can type a letter or write it by hand, but knowing how to structure a letter correctly will make you seem even more intelligent than you really are.

Choose the right type of paper. Yes, the paper matters. You would never write a letter of recommendation on loose-leaf notebook paper, for example.

Your address should be at top of the letter, either in a formal letterhead style (for cover letters and letters of recommendation) or in traditional style of:

Street

City, State, Zip

If it's an informal letter, your address should be right justified. If it's a formal letter, it should be left justified.

The recipient's address should only appear on a formal letter and should be left justified under your address (if your address is not in the letterhead).

The date should be double spaced under your address and right justified in informal letters and under the recipient's address and left justified on formal letters.

The greeting should be left justified and aligned under the date in a formal letter.

The body of the letter should be double spaced directly under the greeting (left justified) and structured into paragraphs. There's no need to indent the paragraphs in a personal letter, and they shouldn't be indented in a formal one either. Be sure to double space between paragraphs.

Your closure should match the formality of your letter. *Sincerely* is usually the best way to close a formal letter. Other options for less formal letters include *yours truly* and *many thanks*, among others.

CHANGE A DIAPER

Whether you become a father or not, you'll probably still find yourself changing a poopy diaper at some point in your life. It might be your nephew or goddaughter, or it could be the son or daughter of a romantic interest. Many men are intimidated by this sometimes messy task, but a real man isn't scared of a little poo.

Place the baby on a safe, clean, soft surface. If you don't have a changing table available, then a couch, bed, or floor will do, but make sure you have one hand on the infant at all times so that they don't roll off. Put a clean towel or cloth under them to protect the surface.

Unfasten the soiled diaper and find out if it's just wet or if it's poopy.

For a wet diaper, fold the diaper underneath the baby's butt so that the outer side of the diaper is now directly under the baby.

Use a baby wipe to wipe the butt and genital area.

For a poopy diaper, use the inside of the diaper to wipe away as much poop from the baby's butt as possible, then fold it underneath the baby's butt so that the outer side of the diaper is now directly under the baby.

Use baby wipes or a warm, wet washcloth to clean the front of the baby. Be sure to get inside all the creases such as where the legs bend at the baby's waist.

Lift the baby's legs up and use baby wipes or a warm, wet washcloth to clean the baby's butt including the crack.

Wipe girls front to back to avoid getting poop in the genital area, which can lead to infection.

Boys often pee when their genital area is exposed to the air. Keep a clean diaper or clean cloth over the genital area any time you remove their clothes. Be sure to clean around the penis and scrotum, and point the penis down when you put the new diaper on to prevent soaked shirts and leaks.

Keeping the legs lifted, pull out the soiled diaper and put a clean, open one under the baby.

Rub any rash creams the baby needs at the time directly onto the skin.

Fold the diaper up so that you have an equal amount of diaper under the baby and on top of the baby.

Pull the sides of the diaper up over the front flap and either pin them down or use the tape flaps to secure the diaper.

Throw out the dirty diaper in a designated diaper pail or trash can. Don't flush the diaper down the toilet.

Dress the baby and wash your hands.

GET SERVICE
AT A BAR

When you go to a bar, getting a drink quickly is kind of the point, but if the bar is packed, it's sometimes difficult for the bartender to see and get to everyone in a timely manner. If you just stand there quietly and wait, you'll probably get passed over. If you're loud and obnoxious, bartenders might purposely ignore you. There is a middle ground, however, that will get you served as quickly as possible.

Don't wave money at the bartender. They're not strippers, and they may find it disrespectful that you think they will serve you faster than other people if you show them the money. (Hint: They won't.)

Instead, lift your hand slightly when the bartender turns your way. They will usually acknowledge you with a nod and finish what they're doing before serving you, but at least you'll know you've been seen.

Don't tell the bartender that it's your turn to be served. Whether you were next or not, bartenders can't always keep track of who showed up to the bar first. They're human, and it's busy. Give them a little slack and know that you'll get better service if you're patient.

Let the ladies go first. Even if you've been standing at the bar for a while waiting to be served, if a woman walks up, let her order before you. Bartenders love good manners and they'll remember you the next time.

Other behaviors that will move you to the back of the line include playing on your phone, demanding free drinks or discounts, and standing in the wrong part of the bar. If you think you're getting passed over, try moving to another spot.

Order all the same drink at one time as it's much more efficient for the bartender to make them together than separately.

Tip well but not excessively. Chances are that the bartender won't notice how much you tipped in a busy bar anyway, so it's not going to make a difference in your level of service.

DEALING AND PLAYING CARDS

Even if you're not much of a gambler, knowing how to deal and play a few card games is basically Man 101. You'll probably have numerous opportunities to play cards with friends, and that's where you'll learn the basics. If you go to Las Vegas or any of the many other gambling sites in the world, these basics will be critical. Even though you can learn while you're there, you're likely to lose a lot of money in the meantime.

Dealing for poker:

There are as many ways to deal cards as there are cards in a deck (52 without the jokers), so we'll discuss dealing for a game of poker as it's a common game among male friends.

> **Shuffle the deck or decks of cards** at least four times. Learn a bridge to make shuffling look more impressive and professional.

Box the cards. Take the top quarter of the shuffled deck and put it on the table. Take the next quarter of the deck and put it on top of the first. Follow this with the third quarter and the last quarter.

Cut the cards. Have a player use the cut card to slice the deck in two portions. Move the bottom portion of the deck on top of the second portion.

Deal the cards starting with the first player on your left and moving clockwise around the table. Holding the deck in one hand, pinch the right corner of the card between your thumb and forefinger and flick the wrist to lightly toss the card face down to the player.

Burn and turn the cards. This means discarding the top card after the deal is done. Don't show this card to the players or look at it yourself. Turn the next card over when it's time, which varies based on the version of poker you're playing.

Manage the pot and point to the player whose turn it is to make a decision. Keep track of bets and raises.

When the hand is over, read the hands out loud (those that are still in the pot) and push the pot toward the winner.

Poker hands:

A poker hand refers to the cards under your control at the end of a round or phase. Each card is ranked with ace and face cards holding the most worth and two holding the least worth. The combinations of the cards is important as their values change depending on how they are laid down together.

A pair is whenever you hold two of the same cards. A pair of twos is worth more than a single ace. Whenever you have a pair in your hand, you'll also want to take note of your highest-ranking card. For example, a pair of twos, ace high, means that your highest card is an ace. If another person holds a pair of twos with a ten as their highest card, your hand will beat theirs.

Three of a kind occurs whenever you hold three of the same valued cards. This hand will beat both a pair and two pairs.

A straight is when you have five consecutively ordered cards. For example, your hand may have a two, three, four, five, and six. This is considered a straight. If another person also lays down a straight, you will compare the value of the cards at this point. The cards don't need to have the same suit.

A flush is when your cards share the same suit. For example, you will either hold all hearts or all spades.

A full house is when you hold a pair and a three of the kind.

A straight flush is when your hand has consecutively ordered cards that all share the same suit.

A royal flush beats all other hands. This hand includes an ace, king, queen, jack, and ten of the same suit.

Texas Hold 'Em poker:

Texas Hold 'Em became the most popular version of poker after experiencing a surge in the 2000s.

Each player gets two face-down cards from the dealer. These are called the hole cards.

A button moves around the table so that the dealer changes with each hand.

The two players to the left of the dealer must ante up, or place the minimum bet in the pot, before the cards are dealt. The player immediately to the left of the dealer is called the little blind and the player two spots to the dealer's left is called the big blind. Usually, the big blind makes the first bet and the little blind makes half the big blind's bet.

Each player then places their bets according to their cards. They can call by matching the bet right before them or raise by increasing the bet. Players can also fold their cards, giving up the hand.

The blinds lose their antes if they fold their bets, but no one else loses money if they fold on the first round.

After the first round, the dealer turns over the next three cards on the deck. This is called the flop.

Each player then goes through a new round of betting, raising, or folding, using their two hole cards and the three flop cards to make their decision.

The dealer turns over the next card on the deck. This is called the river.

Each player then goes through another round of betting, raising, or folding, using their best five cards out of the hole, flop, and river to make their decision.

The dealer flips the next card on the deck, which will be the final one. This is called the turn.

Each player goes through as many rounds of betting, raising, or folding as necessary until everyone calls, using their best five cards from their hole cards and all cards on the table to make their decision.

The player with the highest hand gets that round's pot.

Other card games to learn include three-card poker, Omaha poker, Razz poker, 2–7 triple-draw poker, 7-card stud poker, draw poker, blackjack, gin rummy, hearts, spades, and cribbage. If you need a card game for children, you can also try learning games like *Uno*.

RIDE A BIKE

Hopefully, you learned how to ride a bike when you were a kid. It's much easier to do when you're young (and not just because your body is better able to bounce back from falls), but you can still learn to ride one as an adult if you didn't. It's great exercise and an eco-friendly way to get around town. Plus, if your friends (or date) ever want to go on a bike ride, you'll be ready.

Always wear a helmet when learning to ride a bike or riding a bike *period*. It's manly to protect your brain.

Make sure the bike you're learning on fits you well. You should be able to stand over the bike without the top cross bar pressing into you. If there isn't enough space between your crotch and the top cross bar, you may need a smaller bike.

Practice getting on and off the bike. Lean the bike slightly toward you and apply the brakes. Sling the leg closest to the bike over the top cross bar so that you're straddling the bike.

Walk next to your bike and practice applying the brakes so that you know how much pressure it takes to stop. This will give you confidence when you get on the bike.

Practice balancing using the "glide" method. Scoot your bike with your feet and lift your feet off the ground once the bike is moving slowly. This gives you an idea of how to balance on two wheels. Once you can glide for three seconds or longer without putting your feet down to correct your balance, you're ready to begin pedaling.

Keep your eyes up and focused on where you're going instead of any obstacles in your way.

To begin pedaling, start with one foot on the ground and the other foot on the pedal in the two o'clock position.

Push down on the pedal, and as you move forward, put your other foot on the other pedal so that it's ready to push that pedal down when it gets to the top of its cycle.

The faster you pedal, the easier it will be to maintain your balance, but don't go so fast that you lose control.

HOW TO HAGGLE

No one wants to pay more for something when they know they can get a better price. The art of haggling is something men have done for hundreds, if not thousands, of years to make themselves feel better about paying for things they want or need. While negotiating prices isn't something you see every day in Western culture, it is both expected and encouraged in other cultures. That means the price you see is too high in most cases, and haggling is the only way to get the item for less.

Be honest. Let the seller know you're trying to get a better price. It's not worth the hit to your character to lie about why you want a discount.

Timing is everything. The best time of day to haggle is at the end of the business day when there are fewer customers around and the seller wants to make one more sale before closing shop.

Use cash. All-cash sales are a huge motivator for sellers. Pull out what you're willing to pay and let the seller see it. The emotional and visual impact of this move can't be understated. While you might not be able to do this on huge purchases, when you can, you'll have most of the negotiation power in your corner.

Be ready to walk away. Don't let the seller know how much you want the item. If they know that, you won't get the deal you want. Have a bottom line, and if they won't match that, walk away. If they call you back, great. If they don't, that's okay too. You'll find the exact item or one very similar to it somewhere else for a price you want to pay.

Know the power of silence. When the seller gives you a price, don't say anything. Wait. It's awkward, but if the seller breaks first, you're probably going to get a better deal.

Let them know your budget. You might be surprised at how far down a seller will come on a price when they know how much you have to spend. Of course, if you don't know the price in the beginning, don't give them your budget until you know.

Offer a package deal. Tell them for the price they're offering, they need to throw in something else (choose something expensive), which they'll probably balk at. Then say that if they can't meet that demand, they should at least be able to throw in something else or lower the price. It's a great way to get more for the same price, which is basically the same as a discount.

THROW A FOOTBALL

You never know when the guys will want to toss the ol' pigskin around. Don't humiliate yourself by not knowing how to throw a football.

- Put your index finger on your throwing hand closest to the tip of the football but not on the tip.

- Place your middle finger on the top lace.

- Your ring finger should rest between the third and fourth laces from the top.

- Place your pinkie finger between the fifth and sixth laces from the top.

- Your thumb should be on the side of the ball as close to the center from top to bottom as possible.

- Place your feet shoulder-width apart with your non-dominant leg forward.

- Point your front foot toward your target.

- Place your nonthrowing hand on the ball on the opposite side from the laces.

- The ball's starting position should be between your chest and belly button with the bottom point of the ball, or "nose," pointed straight at the ground.

- Pull your arm back, gripping the ball as described above. The nose of the ball should point straight back or slightly downward.

- Keeping your knees slightly bent, lift your front foot to prepare to take a step forward as you let go of the ball. Place your weight on your back foot as you prepare to throw.

- Push your back foot into the ground to give the throw power.

- Keep your head over your back knee to drive the throw.

- Bring your elbow forward first, followed by your wrist. As your wrist comes forward, release the ball.

- At the same time, shift your weight from your back leg to your front leg.

- Follow through by fully extending and rotating your elbow.

- Your final position should have your arm fully extended with your thumb pointed down and inward.

DRIVE IN BAD WEATHER

No matter where you live, you're going to have to deal with bad weather at some point when you're behind the wheel of a car. Knowing how to drive safely in all types of weather will give your passengers confidence that you'll get them where they're going in one piece. It has the added bonus of keeping *you* alive as well.

Slow down. You might not think it's very manly to drive slowly, but it's better than not arriving at your destination at all. It's hard to control or stop a vehicle in poor weather when you're speeding.

Leave plenty of stopping distance. Increase the distance between you and the vehicle in front of you so that you can safely stop even if you begin to slide.

If there's standing water, don't drive through it. Turn around and go another way or back where you came from. Many people drown in water that they think they can drive through. It's not worth taking the chance.

Be extra cautious of pedestrians, motorcycles, and bicycles since it gets harder to see when it's snowing or raining.

If it's snowing, be aware that bridges and overpasses ice up first because of the cold air passing beneath them. Slow down even more when driving over these structures.

Turn on your wipers or allow your automatic wipers to take over.

Turn your headlights on. Again, you want to be as visible as possible.

Don't turn your headlights on bright when it's foggy. The light will just reflect off the fog and blind you.

If you start to slide, don't hit your brakes. Turn into the slide by turning your wheels in the same direction that the back of the vehicle is sliding. Don't panic or overcorrect.

CONCLUSION

When all is said and done, the skills every man should know are not just about practicality but also about personal growth, self-awareness, and empowerment. By learning these essential skills, you'll gain the confidence and competence you need to navigate life's challenges and achieve your goals.

From fixing a leaky faucet to negotiating a salary, the skills outlined in this book will equip you with the tools you need to succeed in all areas of life. Mastering these skills will allow you to become more self-sufficient, adaptable, and resilient.

Beyond just learning new skills, this book is about becoming the best version of yourself. Exploring your values, strengths, and weaknesses prepares you to make decisions that align with your goals and aspirations.

In short, the skills every man should know are not just a set of practical abilities but a pathway to ongoing learning. Whether you're a young man just starting out or a seasoned adult looking to enhance your skill set, this book is a valuable resource that will help you achieve your goals and live a fulfilling life.

www.ingramcontent.com/pod-product-compliance
Lightning Source LLC
Chambersburg PA
CBHW060237030426
42335CB00014B/1498